Dear Laura

Also by Laura Hird

Nail and Other Stories
Born Free
Hope and Other Urban Tales

Dear Laura

Letters from a Mother to her Daughter

Laura Hird & June Hird

CANONGATE

Edinburgh · New York · Melbourne

First published in Great Britain in 2007 by
Canongate Books Ltd, 14 High Street,
Edinburgh EH1 1TE

1

Copyright © Laura Hird, 2007

The moral right of the author has been asserted

'Coat' by Vicki Feaver, published in *Close Relatives* by
Secker & Warburg (1981). Reprinted with permission.

'He Wishes for the Cloths of Heaven' by WB Yeats,
published in Wordsworth Editions Ltd in
The Collected Poems of WB Yeats (2000). Reprinted with permission.

British Library Cataloguing-in-Publication Data
A catalogue record for this book is available on
request from the British Library

978 1 84195 899 6 (13-digit ISBN)
1 84195 899 9 (10-digit ISBN)

Typeset by Palimpsest Book Production Ltd,
Grangemouth, Stirlingshire

Printed and bound in Great Britain by Clays Ltd, St Ives plc

www.canongate.net

For my dad, Ronnie Hird, and other absent friends

Coat

Sometimes I have wanted
to throw you off
like a heavy coat.

Sometimes I have said
you would not let me
breathe or move.

But now that I am free
to choose light clothes
or none at all

I feel the cold
and all the time I think
how warm it used to be.

Vicki Feaver

Contents

Introduction: A Constipated Romantic   xi

1988: Out of the Frying Pan, Into the Fire   1

1989, Part One: I Love You All Too, And Make
Good Soup   33

1989, Part Two: The Twilight Zone   83

1990, Part One: Come Back Little Sheba   101

1990, Part Two: How Can I Be More Clever
When I'm Already a Genius?   137

1991: The Birds Will Be Building Their Nests
in My Bras   147

1992: Nothing Is Too Hard to Share   171

1992–1997: 10,000 Questions   181

1997–1999: No Best Time of Day   199

Dear Mum   211

Appendixes

Characters   219

Further Writing   230

Acknowledgments   241

A CONSTIPATED ROMANTIC

Introduction

The relationship we have with our mothers is perhaps the most intense of any in our lives. To be created and grow within someone for nine months and to be nurtured after our birth is the greatest privilege we have as human beings. If we have that, we have everything. But it is also a relationship fraught with contradiction and confusion because of its intensity. We all have mothers. We love them, we fight with them, we resent them, we feel guilty for resenting them, we tell them the things that only mothers get excited about.

I hope this book will comfort anyone who is going through the anguish of adolescence, whether as a child or parent; anyone suffering or having to watch a loved one suffer from an illness; the bereaved; anyone who has argued or fallen out with siblings or a best friend; anyone who has to deal with being far away from the people they love – either in distance or emotionally. It is dedicated to anyone who has ever had to let go of the thing they love most.

From as far back as I can remember my mum had a

compulsion to communicate – whether through conversation, sharing literature, writing letters, acting or listening to music in the communal solitude of a concert hall. Even while I was still in the womb, she told me she used to read me poetry, play me her favourite records and sing to me. From my infancy she took great pleasure in nurturing me with books and music. My childhood is awash with memories of her reading me books and poems: Browning's *Pied Piper of Hamelin*, for which I still have the original beautifully illustrated book by Kate Greenaway, and John Masefield's 'Cargoes' which was one of the most exotic things I had ever heard. I loved being able to visualise each ship through the rhythm and pace alone, from the mysterious and beguiling 'Quinquireme of Nineveh from distant Ophir' to the strange relief I used to feel when the 'dirty British coaster' turned up at the end. Mum used to encourage me to use all my senses when I was listening to it and I can still remember the images it conjured.

Alfred Noyes' 'The Highwayman' was another poem that engulfed all my senses. Mum, as a frustrated actress, used to read this in a way that was almost cinematic. The sounds of the horses' hooves ('Tlot-tlot; tlot tlot') growing gradually louder each time the Highwayman approached and the cracking of his whip set against the warm earthiness of language used when Bess is being described were addictive. All these wonderful images and the passion and romance of it all

I just loved. I always cried, as did mum, when the high-wayman died at the end, emotionally drained from the intensity with which she'd read it. The landlord's black-eyed daughter, Bess, had a lot to answer for.

I remember mum reading me Burns' 'Tam o' Shanter' for the first time when I was learning to recite 'To a Mouse' for the Burns Competition at primary school and it feeling like the first real 'adult' piece of writing I'd ever experienced. The wicked relish with which Burns describes all the grotesque items Tam sees lying on the 'haly table' and the part when his horse gets its tail pulled off used to make me scream for mercy, before begging mum 'again'.

Robert Louis Stevenson's poem 'The Land of Counterpane' from *A Child's Garden of Verses* I'll always associate with a hand-stitched quilt that mum and dad inherited when dad's mum died. It was a rose-coloured nylon. Dad used to have to get up early to leave for his work at the brewery at Sighthill at six each morning (to walk the three or so miles there before buses ran that early). He'd come through and give me a kiss on the way out, then I'd run through to spend the next few hours under the quilt in the 'big bed' with mum. It also reminds me of pretending to be ill so I could stay off school under the 'land of counterpane' in mum and dad's bed, daydreaming, just as mum had loved to read it when she was suffering from childhood rheumatic fever, and similarly physically, but not imaginatively confined. Stevenson's own childhood illness had been his inspiration for writing the poem in the first place.

Other favourites were M.C. Smith's 'The Boy on the Train', more commonly known as 'The Next Stop's Kirkcaldy' which we would recite on the way over to Burntisland and Kirkcaldy for the yearly fairs on the Links there. We could eventually time it so we were actually going under the tunnel at the line, 'We're into the tunnel! We're a' in the dark! But dinna be frichtit, Daddy.' And Hilda Boswell's *Treasury of Poetry* ('Leery the Lamplighter', 'Mrs Peck-Pigeon', 'They Went to Sea in a Sieve' and 'The Wraggle Taggle Gypsies') again, illustrations I can still see clearly and words I hear mum reading to this day. The poem 'No Telephones in Heaven' from L.P. Hartley's *Five-Minute Recitations* used to make me cry for hours, as the telephone was always a big part of mum's life and I couldn't bear to imagine a time that she might not be there any more.

Mum and dad were both compulsive readers. Dad used to go to Fountainbridge Library for them every Tuesday on his way back from work and return with a dozen or so books which they would devour and exchange thoughts about over the following week. They always used to enjoy having a few books on the go at the same time. Dad knew exactly the kinds of things mum liked. One of his greatest pleasures was discovering newly published books that mum hadn't had the chance to hear about yet. They also used to enjoy exchanging their favourites – mum's – biographies of actors, singers, conductors and books about old Edinburgh and Scottish history, plus collections of poetry she'd pick up at jumble sales and second hand shops, and dad's − crime fiction, Pan books of horror stories and his all-time favourite, the classic Glasgow gang novel *No Mean City*.

Mum made sure I knew how to read before I started primary school aged four. Through taking the occasional boarder in the front room, and dad doing odd-jobs in the evenings at Cam and Jim's (family friends who run a guest house in the centre of town), mum was able to give up work when I was born until I was eight. She was therefore able to spend time each day reading and teaching me to read from the beautifully illustrated books I've mentioned. With her encouragement I had my first poem published in the *Evening News*'s Junior News when I was five and she was forever uncovering writing and painting competitions for me to enter, in which I was quite successful. (Possibly, I thought, because I was the only kid entering them.) Sometimes, if I felt more inclined to play Scalextric or Action Man with my friend, Mark, next door, dad and she would collaborate instead. Dad was an enthusiastic amateur artist and mum would hone his more elaborate style then add her own touches to produce poster-paint pictures reminiscent of her favourite artist, L.S. Lowry. One of dad's proudest solo projects in my name was a competition to design a dinosaur. Here, given free reign by mum he produced a lavish dragon who they named the 'Hirdigorous' which was featured on sweetie cigarette cards at the time.

In the numerous competitions I/we entered over the years I won bikes, toys, helicopter flights, tape recorders, John Menzies book tokens, singing Sindy dolls, wristwatch radios and, on one occasion, my dream come true – the chance to meet the Scottish entertainer Jimmy Logan, who I'd developed a crush on after seeing him in pantomime and listening to mum's Harry Lauder records. Mum chummed me along to meet him, he was a charming man, and he subsequently sent us a Christmas card each year for the rest of his life. He also gave us a lucky rabbit's paw which mum cherished and would always stroke for luck when she was at a low ebb. I remember the first time I met Jimmy Logan, he asked me what my daddy did for a living, and when I told him he worked in a brewery he roared with laughter. I never really understood at the time what the joke was.

Mum always loved acting and the theatre. As a teenager she'd been offered a place to study at the Royal Scottish Academy of Music and Drama in Glasgow but my grandfather would not allow it at the time (despite her having passed all the relevant entrance exams, plus having the Licentiate of the Royal Academy of Music diploma and elocution certificates) as he feared she would be corrupted amongst the bohemians of 1950s Glasgow. Instead, she became involved in various amateur dramatic and light opera groups in Edinburgh.

Although when I was young she used to fill me with stories about her acting days, I expect it must have been frustrating for her to no longer be involved (aside from the occasional 'Young Wives' production in the local church when she'd let me help her learn her lines) as with a young daughter to care for she no longer had the time to get involved with full-scale productions. But again, the actress in her allowed her to bring the poetry and stories she used to read alive for us.

Mum was a consummate story-teller, whether she was reading from a book or recounting some wonderfully rich and vivid tale from her own life. She was also a great 'romancer' so the line between reality and fantasy was often blurred. A former pupil at James Gillespie's school, mum used to swear that the teacher who was the subject of her first crush was Miss Christina Kay, on whom Muriel Spark allegedly based Jean Brodie. By all accounts she was the crème de la crème.

Mum also instilled in me a love of classical music. In her teens, mum was a huge fan of the great lyric contralto, Kathleen Ferrier, who she was lucky enough to see at the first Edinburgh International Festival in 1947. That same year she saw Bruno Walter conducting the Vienna Philharmonic for the first time since his expulsion from Austria. For a fourteen-year-old girl, in love with music, it was an incredibly exciting time. She would scrimp and save her lunch money for seats in the gods during subsequent festivals throughout the late '40s and '50s. I grew up listening to recordings by many of the artists she subsequently saw appear, as she relished recounting tales of the concerts featuring legendary conductors, singers and pianists including Sir John Barbirolli, Fischer-Dieskau, Alfred Cortot and her favourite, Irmgard Seefried.

She loved to tell me about going on dates, in her late teens, with the 'bohemians' she met during the Festival – Roddy McMillan the Scottish actor, Ian McNaughton (who produced the original *Monty Python's Flying Circus* on BBC Two), etc. When I was growing up, mum used to save her pennies and half-pence pieces in an Opera Jar to pay for trips to the opera or theatre for us both; we would go armed with a bottle of red cola, plastic cups and Ovenfresh pies, cut into four and wrapped in a napkin. We would both sing along to our favourite arias, much to the chagrin of the Morningside ladies and culture vultures in the audience.

My parents first met during a night out at the Cavendish Dance Hall in the 1950s. Instantly besotted, dad went to see mum in a play she was acting in at the time, night after night for the rest of its run, inundating her with presents and flowers. In spite of her more 'cultivated' suitors at the time, my dad's determination and devotion eventually won her over. He was honest, hard-working, loyal, reliable and would do anything for her. On one occasion during their courtship, dad bought mum a record, which she was unable to play as her family didn't have a record player. My uncle recalls looking out the window of the family house in Whitson one night and seeing dad approaching, Samson-like, with a radiogram over his shoulders, which he'd borrowed and carried from his own mother's house in Wardlaw. Mum and dad were married by Reverend Harry Whitley in St Giles Cathedral on 30 April 1960. They then had a one night honeymoon at Peebles Hydro in the Scottish Borders. Dad was a great romantic and put mum on a pedestal. Every week he would spend most of his pocket money (mum gave him £5 from his weekly wage for himself) on bars of tablet, bottles of wine, packets of her favourite sweeties, flowers . . .

From my infancy I remember mum writing letters. The house was always packed to the gunwales with various notelets and brightly coloured writing paper. She made many friends over the years with boarders from around the world who would come back to stay year after year. Her most memorable and enduring correspondence was with Jim, a widower from Kent, with whom her long-time obsession with J.M. Barrie's *Peter Pan* could really fly. Mum had always been a Wendy looking for her Peter. They were both compulsive letter-writers and for years kept each other's spirits up through a postal Never Never Land, often sending each other several long letters a day full of photos, poems and dreams. In these letters to Jim mum could live in a fairytale world, hiding from the harsher realities of life. In her subsequent letters to me, which form the core of this book, she could talk to me as the daughter and friend I'd been before the surliness and confusion of adolescence kicked in and I'd started to reject the fairy stories to search for my own reality.

Mum also shared a passion with her own father for the Lawnmarket where they both grew up. She was an unofficial guide to the many tourists who stayed with us for B&B over the years. She was immensely proud of the fact that she had been born in her beloved granny's flat, in Deacon Brodie's Close. And of the fact that her auntie Theresa lived in a flat overlooking Greyfriars Kirkyard – an area originally known as Bedlam, which had housed one of the city's biggest poorhouses and a lunatic asylum (the neo-Gothic church there now home to the University's Bedlam Theatre Company). It tickled her pink to tell people that she was born in the same close as Dr Jekyll and Mr Hyde and brought up in Bedlam.

My grandfather's memories about the Lawnmarket in the 1920s were somewhat harsher but, like mum's, fascinated me from an early age. He used to fill notebooks and my young imagination with his stories, anecdotes and facts and figures about the place: tales of the women's lodging houses where the inhabitants slept during the day then went out soliciting at night; of the two competing pawnshops in Fisher's Close where families would pawn their bedclothes on Monday mornings to pay for food, then only be able to redeem them on a Saturday morning if the men managed to not spend it all in the pub on payday. Pappa could remember whole families he grew up with being wiped out by tuberculosis which was rife amongst the tenements due to overcrowding, poor sanitation and the fact that ordinary working people could not afford doctor or hospital fees at the time (most families relying on the Livingstone Dispensary in the Cowgate which was run by student doctors who attended patients for free and sold medicine cheaply). I loved his tales of the early Italian and Polish immigrants, the latter making a living from dancing bears in the Grassmarket, with a monkey on a rope that used to climb up to the high tenement windows collecting money in a tin. I found pappa's stories of the squalor and poverty of early twentieth-century Edinburgh a fascinating juxtaposition to my mother's rich tales of the history, royal scandals and ghosts of the same area.

Pappa's family was more fortunate than many of their neighbours. His father was a blacksmith, earning £3 a week, and was also a brass bandsman. Pappa, in turn, after the war, became a blacksmith and bandsman. I was incredibly close to my grandfather when I was young and we used to go to brass band competitions in Princes Street Gardens, the miners' gala days, marches in Princes Street and drink clandestine lemonades at the door of the Wheatsheaf pub while he went in for a fly whisky. Like his daughter, he was an incredibly creative man, loved poetry and music and was proud of his part in a living, growing history. We used to go for long walks along the old railways of

Edinburgh, collecting buckets of 'sheep's pirls' for his garden. In those days herds of sheep were taken to the slaughterhouse at Longstone via the wild, unkempt pathways and there were always easy pickings for his compost heap.

At the start of the 1950s Sean Connery's father used to work for my grandfather, installing fireplaces. On hearing that Connery was also interested in acting (he was in the chorus of *South Pacific* at the time) my grandad suggested to mum that she might be interested in him. On visiting the Connery house in Grove Street with both fathers mum found Sean in the back garden working out (body-building being his other passion at the time). Mum immediately deemed him 'too common'. I find this story hilarious, as mum was never a snob. But I guess, if she had gone on to become the real Miss Moneypenny, then I'd never have been born.

After mum died, re-reading and sharing the letters she'd written to me over the years along with her own archive of letters, cards, stories, poems and holiday diaries gave me great comfort. When I read extracts to friends it felt like she was still there, alive in her own words. They were full of wisdom, life lessons and love that I realised held great meaning, not just for me, but for anyone who had the chance to read them.

The main body of letters featured in this book, namely those mum wrote to me when I was studying down in London in the late '80s/early '90s perhaps resonate most as they are from the only time during her life when we were physically apart. Those letters emotionally sustained both myself and my fellow students with their advice, humour, affection and regular food, new clothes from the catalogue and parcels of toiletries. Reading them out amongst my friends helped them cope with their own homesickness, and the subsequent laughter and tears they elicited proved strangely cathartic to us all. It was as if she was there, mothering and smothering us. When mum used to phone the flat I shared, I'd often not know it was her for ten minutes as my flatmates (who very quickly felt like they knew her) would chat away, confiding in her about their own lives and asking her about hers.

I also love these letters because they detail a very specific part of modern history – the rise and fall of Margaret Thatcher (Thatcher was my local MP when I stayed in East Finchley in 1990), the overhauling of the NHS, the poll tax riots, Pavarotti in the Park, etc. They bring the late '80s and early '90s vividly back, from the death of John Smith, to the death of Brian Tilsley on *Coronation Street*.

In the other letters and extracts included, the theme of distance, and the need to bridge it in its many guises is always present. From the juxtaposition of mum writing to me when I was away from home, to her considering home when on holiday, to the distance a child tries to drive between themself and their parents when they are trying to hide the fact that things are going very wrong in their life; the distance a mother feels when her child refuses to confront problems and the ultimate distance of death.

When I read them now, I can also see starkly, in a way that I could not, or chose not to, at the time, mum's health deteriorating as the years passed. As a child I would often spend the night with grandma and pappa, or across at my auntie Morag's when mum was unwell or had to go into hospital. Most of my happy holiday memories include points at which mum would become ill, from her developing pleurisy while we were in Blackpool, to swollen ankles brought on by long bus and car journeys which often led to mum going into heart failure by the time we returned home. Holidays were always a joy of mum's but invariably they ended up with her suffering from exhaustion and gravely ill upon our return. Any undue stress would make mum breathless, and cause palpitations and chest pains (which were eventually diagnosed as angina). These terrified me as a child, scared she could be taken from me at any moment, and tortured me as a teenager after a relative told me, if mum died it would be my fault. Sometimes I suspected that aspects of her compulsive sense of drama were at play and that not all such attacks were completely genuine; that she was exaggerating the symptoms in a desperate bid to extinguish animosity and confrontation brought on by my adolescent need to pull free of the umbilical cord. In retrospect I realise that part of my own mechanism for coping was to deny to myself how ill she really was, and in turn how much this must have added to the hurt and fear mum must have been feeling.

It was always mum's dream for me to be successful in some creative and fulfilling way. She also wanted me to have the security, stability and social acceptability that a steady job and loving husband, family and friends offer. Like most mothers she longed for me to fulfil her dreams, and to do what ill-health and lack of confidence prevented her achieving herself. When my first collection of short stories was published by Canongate Books (based in the Royal Mile where she grew up) mum and dad were both incredibly proud. They both came to an early reading I did in a gallery in Blackfriars Street, just off the Royal Mile itself, dressed in their Sunday best. Mum declared at the end, 'I really like this Laura. It's a whole new scene.' She used to ask me if I'd write a book about her one day. She hated the possibility that when she died, all her stories, dreams and anecdotes would be forgotten. And that, as I have no children myself, I would have no-one to pass them on to. Sadly, she underestimated just how much those stories had meant to everyone she'd shared them with over the years – myself, friends, my cousin's children, 'pen-pals' and just how enduring and evocative they were.

Since mum died, every time I revisit the letters, they bring her very much alive. Her affection, frustration, wicked sense of humour, strength and encouragement.

They comfort me and inspire me and make me feel very human. There is nothing in these letters that has not been felt or experienced by any mother and child. They express that thing called unconditional love.

1988

Out of the Frying Pan, Into the Fire

On leaving school, I began a course in secretarial studies
(the only exam I'd failed at school) at Stevenson College.
I only lasted three months. This was followed by a disastrous stint as an office assistant for a Chartered
Surveyors, then after many failed job applications and
interviews, I started working as an office junior for a
civil engineering company in the West End of Edinburgh.
The wages were poor, but it gave my life some much
needed structure. I was able to pay mum a paltry amount
of digs money and it meant I was free from the soul-
destroying business of applying for jobs unsuccessfully
at last. The office manager, Rosalind, whose son I had
known at school, became someone I could share some
of the problems I didn't want to worry mum with, but
like mum, she had to put up with my moods, hangovers,
increasingly wayward behaviour and bad temper. It was
certainly not the Civil Service job that mum had always
planned for me, but I learned the ropes, got on with it
and spent a great deal of time typing long letters to my
friends on the (then) luxury of an electric typewriter.

At weekends I carried on my Saturday job from school at Rae Macintosh classical record shop for a bit of extra money. Any money I earned that didn't go on my bus pass or digs money, I spent on going to the cinema or to pubs and clubs with my friends Anne (a friend from school) or Alan (who worked in Rae Mac's with me) at weekends. When my wages would run out a week after being paid, I'd borrow from mum, Rosalind, anyone who would lend me money. Then, when their patience ran out, I arranged overdrafts and secured a credit card.

Mum, at the time, was working, as she had done since I was eleven, as a medical secretary for the Polwarth Medical Practice. Mum adored the job. Over the course of her life she'd worked for Duralay, at the Ideal Homes Exhibition, sold Kleenex hankies to soldiers on Edinburgh Castle esplanade and in the hormone laboratory at the Usher Institute. (Mum used to tell me that all the girls she worked with there, like her, took years to conceive, whilst ironically working in the field of reproductive medicine. Then around the time mum fell pregnant, they all did. She used to joke that it was them who had discovered artificial insemination.) However, it was her work at the doctor's surgery that she really loved as she revelled in the rich mix of people she met – the doctors, reps, old ladies with their life-stories, junkies, mothers with their children, transsexuals, alcoholics. They were all fodder for her stories and anecdotes. The work was stressful, particularly when she had to cover other people's shifts, deal with changes in the NHS, or when the computer system was first put into place, but she loved the challenge and relished garnering the respect of the GPs.

Dad worked as a stock-keeper and clerk for Alloa Brewery from 1963 until 1987 when he was made redundant following a merger. After twenty-four years of manual work in a job he loved, it was hard for him to adapt to applying for jobs and attending interviews again whilst temping in-between times. He worked a contract as an audit clerk with the Royal Bank of Scotland for a while, then found a clerical job with the investment firm, the WM Company. A shy, retiring man, with his confidence further knocked from the redundancy, he found it difficult to fit in to the new environment with young, ambitious and unfamiliar colleagues. But he put his head down and got on with it for mum's and my sake, even though it was obvious he was unhappy.

I'd hoped when I started working that I'd be able to move into a flat. As the months and years went by and my wages lasted less and less of the month, this became a distant dream. The extremely close relationship I'd had with mum when I was young began to stifle me more and more. We argued frequently, over her opening my mail, my staying out late, my choice in boyfriends, my drinking, increasing surliness and anger at anyone and everyone. The arguments would leave mum and dad exhausted and devastated and me guilty and even more angry. I hated having to listen to lodgers in the next room, arguing, making love, talking in loud foreign accents, even though these same lodgers were the ones whose money kept us going and ensured I always had new clothes or could borrow from mum the day after I got paid. My mum's friend, Margaret, would often act as a mediator, taking me out for coffee, letting me cry on her shoulder then trying to resolve problems between my parents and myself. I didn't know what it was I wanted to do. I just knew I didn't want to continue doing what I was doing.

In summer 1988, when I was twenty-one years old, my friend Alan and I decided that the only way we were going to ever get any sort of independence (he lived with his parents in Livingston and travelled through to Edinburgh to work each day – often staying over at our house) was to apply to university. Alan was interested in art – we'd both just completed Higher Art at night class at the Wester Hailes Education Centre – and I, initially, fancied librarianship. I had a fondness for libraries having spent most of my time at high school hiding in one to avoid the bullies.

Mum was encouraging about my sudden interest in higher education. However, after my previous disastrous attempt doing secretarial studies at college, she was concerned that I wouldn't be able to stick at any subsequent course. Despite this though, she phoned around and got me application forms from all the local universities and colleges. I didn't get into any of them.

Both Alan and I applied to Aberystwyth University. His application was successful. My own, including the other universities I'd selected on the UCCA form, was rejected. My friend Anne had recently gone to live and study in Paris. I couldn't bear the thought that Alan might soon be leaving too, leaving me stuck in Edinburgh by myself. Even my youngest cousin Nicola was about to start studying at Edinburgh University.

I subsequently went into the university clearing system and was offered a place at Middlesex Polytechnic. I had hoped for Kingston, as that was where my friend Bob lived at the time, and I thought at least there'd be someone there I knew. As it turned out, I'd read a lot more into that potential relationship than was really there.

Mum and dad were proud and tentatively delighted that I'd finally tried for something and got it. I think they were both shocked when I immediately wrote back and accepted the place on the course, though. Mum said I hadn't thought about it enough, but because I'd been given the place through clearing, time was already running out to find accommodation and I was too late to find a place in halls on campus.

I started buying *Time Out* from the newsagents in Waverley Station and studying the lists of flats to rent in London. I'd only ever visited London once, for the day, when I had been on holiday with mum and dad to see mum's friend, Jim, in the early 1980s. I had no concept of what a huge place it was.

The rents all seemed to be extortionate and required a deposit and a month's rent in advance. I had no idea how far various districts were from Tottenham, where I was to be studying in my first year. Arranging to view a number of flats that I'd phoned up about in *Time Out*, I got the overnight coach down to Victoria, booked to return the following night. The journey was hellish, with drunken squaddies either snoring or yelling at each other, and a stop-off at a motorway service station in the middle of the night during which a mouse dropped on me from steps above and then died at my feet. I got no sleep and arrived in London at seven o'clock the following morning, utterly exhausted.

With my habitual lack of common sense or priority, my first stop when I got there was all the way out to Heathrow to meet Bob for lunch. I had imagined this would take about twenty minutes on the tube. By the time I arrived and had got some idea of just how far things in London were apart, I was starting to panic. Next stop was back across the other side of the city to Wood Green to view a flat that a group of lesbians were sharing. (I figured I would be less likely to get into trouble if there were no men there.) When I emerged at the tube station at Wood Green it seemed like I was the only white person. Having never been in such a situation before, despite having grown up in a city I'd always thought was fairly cosmopolitan, I found it incredibly intimidating; as if I'd suddenly woken up on another continent. I tried asking a few people for directions but my pleas were repeatedly ignored. It felt as if no-one else could actually see me, which intensified my feeling of paranoia and being completely out of my depth. When I attempted to locate the flat myself and realised I was lost, a massive panic attack ensued. I ended up back at Victoria Coach Station by late afternoon, crying and hysterical on the phone to mum saying I wanted to come home. I assume at this point she thought I'd seen sense.

But when I got home, my desire to make it in London had survived my ordeal. It was terrifying but exciting. I began hunting for accommodation again. A friend of mum's told her about a Methodist hostel in Muswell Hill where their son had once stayed. Mum got in touch with them, and thanks to a reference from a family friend (taking the moniker Reverend for the occasion) I was offered a place. This was not what I had planned. No friends allowed to stay overnight, no people of the opposite sex allowed in your room at any time of the day (most of my friends were male), and it looked to be miles from the polytechnic. Determined still to go to London I agreed, only to be saved by the bell when someone pulled out of halls in the week before I moved down and I was offered their place instead. I was set.

The opening letter from mum was given to me between the point of being offered the place in the Methodist hostel and getting the place in halls. I think it is a good place to start the book. This book is about

7

letting go of the thing you love most, about letting people grow and about the difficulties and contradictions the whole process throws up. Despite her fears and reservations, even within the course of this first letter, mum started to come round to the idea of me going away and even set up a Bond with some of their savings, the interest from which she sent me each month to help me out financially.

5 September 1988

[*On envelope – To Laura*]

Please read this right through, when you have time. Sorry if the beginning is hard but it is important that you take stock of yourself before you go to London.
I love you and always will or I would not waste my time.
Good luck for your future.
Love Mum

[*Letter*]

Dear Laura,
You will not speak or communicate with me – only give me a pack of oaths and insults and use every form of emotional blackmail of which you are capable and you know the things which hurt the most and use them. I am afraid I am no longer fit or able to argue with you, as it leaves me feeling physically drained at a time that I should

8

be leading as serene a life as possible. However, I will not play the 'Hearts and Flowers' to you as it would be a wasted effort anyway.

However I would not waste my time or effort writing this if I did not care. God alone knows why I still do but I always shall and will do until the day I die. You always seem to confuse caring with interfering and believe me there is a vast difference. I know now I should have been stricter with you when you were younger and later on. Perhaps you would have grown up with a little consideration for others, been less self-indulgent, taken greater care of your personal appearance and looked after the things you had. I stupidly went out and replaced the things you lost and destroyed, paid for any whims you fancied and when the whim wore off, paid for the next whim and the next one. Perhaps if you had been forced to pay for your own whims and replace the things you destroyed you would have appreciated them more but I am sure my indulgence has contributed greatly to making you the selfish girl you are. I am sure your friends would agree with me that you are selfish and stupidly pig-headed and wilful.

Having got that off my chest, I do not want to waste any more valuable time on recriminations because the issue in hand is probably the most important one in your life, as your whole future is at stake. I know you are capable of succeeding, because you have the intelligence to make it to the top but I wish my faith in your intelligence was matched by my faith in your maturity and application to hard work. However, I am optimistic that given the right goal to strive for you will apply yourself and grow up once the apron-strings and umbilical cord are cut.

I am sure when you think about it, you will agree with the worries which are tearing me apart at the present moment. The first few months in a strange town are difficult enough. In London it will be more difficult. You will be on your own for the first time in your life (except for Bob). Accommodation in London is expensive. In a flat or bed-sit you can be very lonely until you make friends, and that can take time. You have a safe cocoon of nice friends, who have learned to put up with your moods – high and low – and <u>care</u>. And although you feel you despise us and long to escape from parental tyranny you have always been sure of a warm roof over your head, clean clothes, food to eat, hot water to wash in, and hand-outs when you are hard up, which was often (another worry!!). By saying this please don't think I am trying to put you off going to college – believe me I am so happy that you are at last <u>attempting</u> to think positively again.

The minister on Saturday said 'Love is knowing when to let go.' I felt that message was for me. I shall miss you and your calls in the afternoon – 'Any letters?' – our very rare little chats in the wee small hours when I felt very close to you. The joy I have had in the past year hearing you play the piano again and joining us for a video or chatting when Ian and Alan called. We seemed to have broken through a barrier at last. However, I still had to let go <u>because</u> I love you and you had too much intelligence to stagnate as you have done for the past few years.

Letting your only child go means that you want to be sure that she is not 'jumping out of the frying pan into the fire'. You want to make sure that she is safe, warm and fed and above all, happy. That her surroundings are pleasant and clean to make study more enjoyable. That there is someone close at hand if she is sick or feeling lonely.

You shout me down when I try to explain this but this is what being a mother is all about.

Surely congenial surroundings and security are more important to being a successful student than whether Bob or Alan can stay the night. You always get your priorities wrong and it has mucked up your life in the past. Please start to grow up by putting your priorities in order of importance. You are being given an opportunity to study a subject you love, it will mean a lot of hard work and application but you are capable if you put that first and foremost on your list of priorities. You can no longer say, 'I will do that tomorrow, next week, next month.' Study must be No. 1 on the list if you hope to graduate.

That is the reason I want you to stay somewhere where your food is cooked, study facilities and washing and ironing provided, plus a piano. A little discipline expected would not be a bad thing in your case. It did not need to be the Methodist one (in spite of what your friend said it was highly recommended by someone who stayed there) and that was the only reason I tried to persuade you.

I have saved a <u>little</u> money from the summer visitors which I hoped Dad and I might have a weekend away before hospital but if you find hostel accommodation I would have given it to you (about £120) but if you do your own thing, you will have to do it alone because I am afraid for you in a flat to begin with.

We are always here, we love you and hope with all our hearts that you will at last find the elusive bird of happiness that has always seemed to escape your grasp. It is all up to you, Laura. You *can* make it I know but don't create difficulties before you start. Try to anticipate the problems ahead before they happen because by the time they do, they are difficult to keep under control.

Love as always and ever,

Mum

P.S. You have to pay a month in advance in a flat and pay full when on holiday.

I moved down to London for the polytechnic freshers week in early September. Dad was temping with Royal Bank of Scotland at that time but mum, Alan (who didn't start at Aberystwyth till the following week), and Bill, our friend from the Art Higher course at Wester Hailes, came to see me off. Margaret had bought me two huge expandable cases which I'd over-filled with books, CDs, my ghetto blaster, duvet, towels, and special pillow I'd had since I was an asthmatic infant.

It was a tearful and emotional parting, with mum proud of what I was doing but I think still hopeful that I'd change my mind at the last moment.

I don't remember feeling nervous on my first train journey down. I was too excited about the prospect that I was actually going to be living in London. I'd had a hugely romantic view of the place for most of my life, through music, films and TV. I listened to Vaughan Williams' 'Greensleeves' and 'Fantasia on a Theme by Thomas Tallis' as the train sped me through the English countryside towards my new life. I didn't know what was in front of me. I just knew that this time I had to make a go of it. Whatever happened, I couldn't go home with my tail between my legs. I couldn't admit I'd done the wrong thing again, even though I knew mum would have welcomed me back with open arms.

I arrived at King's Cross for the first time ever in the middle of the rush hour. After standing in a long queue for a taxi, I was knocked back by several cockney cabbies who ominously said they 'didn't go to Tottenham'. But still, as I remember, no nerves. I just soaked it all up, dazzled to be surrounded by the station and streets I'd seen for years in my favourite films and TV dramas – *Mona Lisa*, *The Firm* . . . relishing the many different accents and skin colours. Looking around for the prostitutes and drug dealers I'd seen in documentaries.

When I finally got up to the halls, registered and got into my room my body was pumping (partly from humping Margaret's huge cases across the green, marking my entrance with two ploughed troughs that led to Devonshire Hall, where I was to be staying). My room seemed huge, had a sanded floor (before every man and his dog had sanded or laminated floors), a big bookcase, my own bed and window that looked out onto the green and the London sky. I opened the window and breathed in the London air, got some music on and felt fantastic. I emptied my cases, put my CDs and books on my bookshelf and my knick-knacks and pictures about the place, tentatively popping into the kitchen twice to make a cup of tea and saying a nervous hello to a couple of fashionably scruffy middle-class teenagers.

The next day at matriculation I got talking to a girl from Dorset called Claire, who lived in my halls. We immediately bonded and are still friends today. I was initially wearing my office garb (sensible skirt, court shoes, pastel-coloured middle-aged blouses) and felt suddenly very old at twenty-one as most of the other students were in their teens. My original attire was quickly replaced by my sloppy-joe trousers and things I used to wear about the house.

That second night I met more of my fellow hall-mates as we all tried to cook for ourselves for the first time. A boy called Alex got everyone's attention and said we should all meet in the kitchen the following night and get drunk to break the ice. The next night we all did. From that point forth I felt completely at home. It felt as if for the first time I had brothers and sisters.

I phoned mum each night from the communal coin box, delighted to be able to tell her it was all going well; delighted that she didn't have to worry about me. I would drag my friends to the phone to confirm to her that everything was fine.

Eleanor, a friend from Donegal who had just graduated from Edinburgh University, came down to see me in my first couple of weeks there. After years of expecting mum and dad to give a bed for the night to my friends at short notice, now I had my own room I suddenly didn't want to share it. I finally had a sense of my own space.

She eventually went home early but before she left I phoned mum and made Eleanor tell her I was OK too. Mum was pleased and relieved for me and day by day the tension in her voice lessened till she too was as excited as I was each night, with so much to tell each other. Communication seemed much easier from a distance. When she'd waved me off on the train at Waverley Station just a week or so before she made me promise that wherever I was, whatever I was doing, to think about her at midnight each day, and that she'd be thinking of me too and sending positive vibrations. For the first few weeks I took great comfort from doing so.

[*I received the following letters when I was in London:*]

5 October 1988

Laura's Highland Home
Wednesday
P.S. A wee pressie enclosed

My Dearest Laura,

Instead of shopping, I decided to catch up on some hand washing, try to make another attempt on the mountain of ironing (which seems to get bigger and bigger every day) and I thought I would drop you a little note to reach you by the weekend (if you have time to collect it).

I bet you were glad to see the back of the 'T'care' girl, Eleanor.[1] I would certainly discourage any future visits from her. I don't think it is a good idea to have friends stay when you have so many studies. You don't really have time and you want to do your best. You have all the time in the world to study, don't waste it. (Anne is different. I don't mean her.)

Nikki seems to be settling down at university now. She still has not absolutely made up her mind on history yet but she studies at the library until 9 p.m. every night and works all day Saturday and Sunday at Safeway. However, she has made a few friends and seems to be accepting the transition from school. I don't suppose she has much choice if she wants to stay at university.

---

[1] Eleanor used to use the expression 'T'care' (take care) a lot to the extent that mum and I started using it as a prefix to her name when she came up in conversation.

Are you feeling it cold in London? Last 2 days have been really frosty here. Quite breaks my miserable heart to have the central heating on about 6 hours a day. Do you need your warm coat sent on? Does the polytechnic have a sweatshirt or scarf? I could get you that for your birthday if you wish. Have you lost any weight on your vegetarian diet? And without mumsie's coconut sludge and puddings? By the way, discovered who ate all the home-made goodies – 3 guesses, yes you are right, the guy who hid them and said you ate them – Dad. Made 2 huge boxes of chocolate fudge slices on Friday. Margaret and Jack had a piece each, I had 2 bits and it's finished. Now where do you think it has gone? It can't be much fun for him. He does not need to hide it now and still it vanishes, greedy b*****.[2] I wonder if he sups condensed milk?

Great news. We had the video fixed and it plays films in colour like everyone else's now. Hope it lasts until Christmas.

Went back to work on Monday after the week's holiday. We did enjoy the break, had lots of nice runs and lunches but I could not sleep at night. I am so used to getting up at 7 a.m. and working under pressure at the surgery. I could not cope with having a lie-in and having all that leisure time. My brain was still wide awake at 3 and 4 a.m.

---

[2] Mum and dad used to have to hide her delicious home-made sweets from me, otherwise I would pick at them and they consequently wouldn't last long.

Don't know what I will be like when the op time comes.[3] I am dreading all that spare time to cope with more than I am the operation. How will I fill in all that spare time? I will write to everyone and surprise them. That should take care of a few hours. Might write a best-seller. Shit, I wish I did not have to get this op. I have so much I want to do and I don't have time but then I had better get it over with before Maggie Thatcher finishes off the National Health Service and charges for ops too. Apparently I will only get a few days' warning for the op. I hope it is not before Christmas.

Enough about me. I am glad you are still enjoying London. We miss you but I have adapted surprisingly well to 'having a daughter studying in London' especially as you are coping well and doing what you always wanted to do.

How is Virginia Woolf? Don't leave it until the last minute like you usually do. You would have loved Jack's sister, Sylvia Secker. She knew everyone in the literary world when her husband was alive. 'Oh Virginia, she and her husband, Leonard, were great friends of Richard Kennedy, who was visiting me last week. Virginia loved dancing and would have loved the Hammersmith Palais but the Bloomsbury Set would not have approved.' Jack was telling her about you. You should have heard him, you wouldn't have got your hat on. 'Laura is an unusually gifted

---

[3] Mum was on an NHS waiting list for a mitral valve replacement for several years.

girl, a gifted writer, gifted artist, gifted musician, a natural for publishing.'

He, Margaret, Jim and Nannie are your staunch fans. Dear old Nannie was out burning her weekly candles for you and I, and had a bad fall in the street. Poor wee soul. She was bruised all over when we visited her. She said, 'I pray to God to spare me until I see Laura graduated. She will need my candles until then – then He can call me home whenever He wishes.' Splendid old soul she is. The 80–90 year olds are a special breed as we know with Grandma and Pappa. They have twice the guts of younger people (and that includes me – no guts).

Well toots, I want to post this for 5 p.m. T'care and be good (if you can). Work hard. Miss you.

Your loving Mumsie xxx till midnight

23 October 1988

Sunday
Mummy and Daddy Bear's House – Sunday afternoon

Dear Baby Bear,
Did you think Mumsie had forgotten how to write? I don't know where the week went to after you left.

Colin, the boarder, decided to come back for another week last Sunday and now another week. He does not seem to have had much luck at finding a flat or else he is not trying very hard. I am not complaining. He goes home at the weekend and it is giving me a chance to get some cash back in my depleted kitty, even if he is a single. We had another break on Friday. Cam phoned me at the surgery, place full of doctors and patients.

'Can you take a couple and 2 children tonight? – £30.'

I had to answer making it sound like a patient making an appointment. God, my heart was pounding.

'Yes, Mrs O., we can fit you in this afternoon around 4.30 p.m.'

Didn't finish until 3 p.m., sheets needed ironing and table cloth. Had to get Colin's things out of the wardrobe and drawers so that he doesn't know his room was let. A Z-bed to put up, room to hoover and polish. Just made it when they arrived. I was knackered. I have been coping at work with a new girl to train. June on holiday, Elizabeth's left, Jean leaving next week, the cleaner on holiday. Dad and I have been going in at 8 a.m. to clean the surgery.

I had to cope with an afternoon smear clinic on Monday (worked from 8 a.m. until 5 p.m. without a lunch or coffee break) and the same on Tuesday for the baby clinic. I was the only typist there this week so I had 50-odd letters to do. Of course, it was my Saturday on and I had gout in my knee so I don't know how I survived the week. I am on holiday this week, so I hope 3 days' rest will restore me to my former incapacitated state before I come up for my monthly review at Cardiology on Wednesday. I don't want to be dragged in now. I want to be fit when you come home at Christmas. However, I don't want to go in the springtime or summer or autumn either probably.

January would be best but it is cold in January for Dad going home without a tea ready and no clean shirts etc. It is rather like that song from *Camelot*. 'If ever I would leave you, it wouldn't be in springtime.' I always keep hoping that some morning I will wake up and find it's all better but I doubt even Nannie burning every candle in every Catholic church in Edinburgh could achieve that and her magic candles have already blessed us with the greatest miracle – seeing my baby bear settled and happy for the first time in her life and that makes up for any disappointment I have had in life. When my baby is happy, I am happy too.

Yesterday (Saturday) after work, we managed to fit in a jumble sale (any use for a nice, big, fine, pink polo neck jumper?) and a run in the autumn sunshine, carpets of gold and red leaves everywhere – glorious – I love the autumn colours. It makes me wish I could paint, or write poetry or music. You are lucky having all those gifts to express yourself. I am a constipated romantic. I have the emotions within me but I do not have the faculties to express my joy at the glory of nature or my sadness at man's inhumanity to man. I am sure if I had, I could produce a masterpiece but like my darling Daddy, it is all locked up in the heart and soul, but it is comforting to know that the gift (or curse – whichever way you look at it) has been inherited by you and you have the brains and education to use it.

I do drivel on. Apart from the run yesterday, we had afternoon tea in a cute chintzy tea-room in the country.

21

Not posh afternoon tea like we had in Jenner's (that was a happy, special afternoon tea, engraved in my happy memories book to remember anytime I am sad).[4] I felt so close to you, so happy, happy you had grown up so much in 4 weeks. You ordered and <u>paid</u> for <u>my</u> tea and gave me a roll-up. I wanted to shout to all those upper class matrons sipping coffee with clipped Morningside accents, 'This is my daughter, Laura, home from London. You are all going to hear from her someday.' Thank you, darling. Those few hours were precious to your old Mum, who waffles on and on when she writes a letter. Sorry.

Back to yesterday. After afternoon tea yesterday we had 2 Mexican boys present themselves for B&B. God, they looked sweet and spoke like the Cisco Kid or the Three Caballeros in the Walt Disney cartoon. Remember?

'Jose Amigo, no matter where he go, the one, two and three go. We're always together.'

Never mind if you don't remember. You get the picture. They spoke <u>no</u> English except 'disco' and a piece of paper with 'Cinderella Rockafella'. Ian and Alan arrived by this time and Ian took over directions by bus to St Stephen Street, phoned Cinderella to ask what they should wear, how much? They left and returned about midnight with a smile on their faces. After breakfast (cooked by Dad) they said, 'Adios Amigos,' and left us £20 richer. It was hard

---

[4] During the time I'd been home for a week's break I'd taken mum to Jenner's tea room for the afternoon. The first time in my life I can actually remember treating HER.

work this weekend – changing beds, cooking, directing etc., etc., but we made £50. The room is back to a single for Colin's return tonight. Hope he doesn't realise we have been cashing in on his absence. He works with the Inland Revenue!!

Ian and Alan were asking for you as well as Margaret and Jack. I wasn't very pleasant to Ian last night. My Rosé d'Anjou he said was best of the cheapie wines (cheap! – snotty wee bugger and us thinking Concorde at £1.49 a bottle was the crème de la crème). I bought a cream cake at Crawford's, which he said was 'off'. He sat, drinking the despised Rosé d'Anjou, and counted the dead daddy-long-legs in the light shade.

'They are crane flies you snotty little git,' I screamed at him with all the verbal eloquence I could muster.

He looked stunned, laughed and pissed off, surprised that his little sister could react to his sarcasm in such a nasty way. My gouty knee had not helped my temper, but I have never blown my top at Ian before; always kept my sense of humour but he might think twice before being so arrogant again. He and Bob would get on, wouldn't they? Never be a snob, love. Even if you ever have cause to be. It is a nasty trait and usually covering up an inferiority complex.

Well, that's about all our news since you left a week ago. I miss you but don't think it grieves me. I am happier knowing you are fulfilling the gifts you were born with. You were not born with a silver spoon in your mouth but you have many gifts. The silver spoon might make life easier but does not bring happiness that using and fulfilling natural talents bring. It is a lot of hard work but you will make it, my Laura.

Just about another 7 weeks to go and you will be with us again with all your tales. I look forward and work hard to make the time pass more quickly. Have you had your hair cut yet? How is the cooking? Have you written to Jim? Have you done your washing? (End of lectures.)

Write when you can. I enjoy your letters, read them over and over, quote chunks to anyone who is interested. Dad loves them too and misses you but he, like I, is so happy that you will never be caught in the trap that we were, of having too few qualifications.

Fondest love, a hundred kisses until midnight when I say, 'Goodnight Laura and Teddy.' I must stop. I have 6 more letters to write. I should have written them first but they don't give me as much pleasure as writing to you.

Love from Mumsie xxx

21 November 1988

My Dear Laura,
I am sending these off for your birthday and Christmas because it is important to know if they fit and if you like them. If there is anything that doesn't fit or you don't like, please return to me immediately and I mean immediately. I cannot afford to keep anything you don't want anymore. We might manage to get another pair of trousers at Christmas with any birthday money. Hope you like the

gear. If anything needs washed before Christmas, don't wash the new things yourself. I will do it when you are home.

I never get a chance to talk to you these nights. I am longing to hear how the course is doing and how you got on with Alan and Anne. It would be lovely to have a letter some time. I miss you but try to keep myself busy.

Just as well you are not at home. The poll tax for Edinburgh is £420 per person per annum. The highest for the UK.

Please write to Jim as soon as possible. He will send you £5 each month for books but always likes to have it acknowledged and I can't write for you as he would recognise the postmark. It is only polite anyway and he has 5 grandchildren of his own he could give it to, so please Laura, send him a wee note whenever he sends it. He sends cash so that you do not need to worry about cashing a cheque.

I am enclosing the *Scotsman*'s article about Rae Macintosh. Jim says Foyles in Charing X Road is the best place in London for 2nd-hand books but bring your book list home at Christmas and we will keep our eyes open for any at jumbles or book fairs.

Keep your fingers crossed for me on Wednesday. I have my monthly monitoring at Cardiology and they are going to find out when I might be called for my op. I hope it is not before Christmas. I want to be here when you come home and I would like one more Christmas with my old heart, even if it is wonky. I am attached to it and after the op it will be quite a long time before I have much energy again. I am trying to get all my little odds and bobs in order.

I must do some shopping now. Take care, work hard and let me know how you are.

Love Mum xx

24 November 1988

Dear Laura,

I enclose the Bond so that you can cash your cheque.

<u>Please</u> return Bond immediately. I am not very happy about letting it out of my custody as it is the only proof we have to the existence of the £2,000. I will try to come up with some other solution.

I hope you are studying hard, it is nice to have some fun but studying is the main purpose for going to college and you have a golden opportunity which won't come your way again. It is up to you.

Sorry this note is short. I want to get this off quickly and have spent most of today in bed with gout again. Hope you manage to chat a little bit tonight or if you could drop me a little note this week?

It is good, the amount being another £3 this month. I think it may be because October had 31 days. I know you won't but it may be a good idea to hold on to the £3 towards your fare home.

Love Mumsie xxx

[Postman Pat *illustration by mum on note paper*.]

28 November 1988

Dear Laura,

Trousers enclosed – hope they do. They were not on sale but match the set. They look nice. If they are too long perhaps someone would help you shorten. If anything does not fit please return <u>immediately</u> or I will be charged for them. Now remember, you will only get a card on your birthday but you might get a wee thing from Santa if you are a good girl.

I bought you some cheddar cheese in case you want to have a wine or beer and cheese party on your birthday. I also enclose cheese sauce in case you want macaroni cheese & soup course.

It will seem funny you not being here on your birthday – we will be thinking of you and sending our love and it will be only a few more weeks until you are home after all.

Jack took your book list to see if he can pick up some 10p psychology books. He said that an edition of *The Trial* by Kafka was going on sale this week for a record sum for any book. As this sale was at Christie's and not jumbles we decided to leave it for someone else.

However today I got *Vanity Fair*, *Twelfth Night*, *Treasure Island* and a poetry book all for 20p and will keep looking.

Thanks for the Bond and for your letter. Everyone wants to read them. Dad, Margaret and Jack, Ian & Alan.

I must admit I only have one moan now. Write to old Jim if you want another fiver and keep the fivers for books not booze.

I must dash – our video tapes in colour now and I can tape through the night now. Have no time for anything else, nor the inclination.

Love you,

Your loving Mumsie

29 November 1988

My Dearest Laura,

Nannie posted this for you today. I am redirecting it to you immediately. I know how you are about writing thank-you notes and have written one, addressed it and stamped it. Do you think you could post it right away for the London postmark? But please write Jim's one yourself and don't forget to bring his typing home.[5] I noticed Nannie enclosed a fiver. Thought you might like to buy a book you need down there or something else, instead of getting a book token with it.

Hope you have a lovely birthday. Miss you.

Hugs, bugs and kisses,

Love Mumsie xxx

---

[5] Mum's friend Jim had asked me to do some typing for him which he was going to pay me a small amount for doing on my portable typewriter.

[*Birthday card from Nannie enclosed: 'To my dear Laura xxx
– Every success in all your undertakings. Hope you are happy
and like where you are. Love from Nannie xxx'*]

7 December 1988

My Dearest Laura,

Don't faint, a letter at last. So glad you had a happy birthday.
It seemed strange that you were away from home but I
thought a lot about you on the 2nd allowing myself the
luxury of reminiscing about the happiest day of my life, 22
years ago, when I first saw you, already an individual even
then, arriving at tea-time so that your Dad could see you
at the visiting hour and he floated out of Maternity intoxi-
cated without alcohol, stopping strangers in the street
saying, 'I am a Dad. I have a baby girl.' I was so contented
this year knowing that you are well on the way to realising
your full potential. A bright wee baby, a bright wee girl, a
hell of a teenager and now an intelligent, responsible young
woman.

However, enough of that. I have enclosed your cheque
and Bond. (Put the Bond in a safe place and don't forget
to bring it home with you next week.)

I also enclose a birthday card for you to post to Carole
for her birthday on the 9th. Just post it right away like you
did with Nannie's. I have stamped it. I also enclose the
cutting about Woody.[6]

---

[6] Woody Allen – I was a massive fan of his.

Looking forward to seeing you. Colin is still here. I don't like to chuck him out. The cash is handy for Christmas pressies and putting something away for when I am in hospital. He goes away on Thursdays or Fridays and will be away for Christmas and New Year so if he has not found a flat, would you mind sleeping the odd night in the boxroom?

The dresses were all sold from Grattan and Peter Craig. The spring/summer catalogue is out but they are not taking orders until beginning of January 1989. I went along to Evans today. They had nothing. In despair, I went into Marks and Sparks and there it was – a size 24. In black jersey and also in jade green. I took the black but if you would like the green for a change I can swop it.

[Drawing of dress on letter]

It is long with long sleeves, a good skirt, like your black skirt, padded shoulders, low waist and buttoned to the waist and really lovely quality. I bought you a couple of pure silk scarves to brighten it up. I am sure you will love it. It is really you. I did not get you the red sweater as the dress cost a bit more than usual. Try not to burn holes in it. It would be a dress you could wear anywhere, even if you got a wee job.

Ian and Alan were over last night. I was in my bitchy mood again (gout playing me up) and we argued all night.

I have been trying to get Christmas shopping done – murder, shops so busy.

Carole is still preggers, 7 and a half months to go and

everyone having a nervous breakdown already. Nikki has changed to social history as her main subject. To save money she works in the library in the evenings and borrows the books at the weekend. I think most of her grant must still be intact in the bank. It'll be handy for the yearly family trip to Disneyland!

However, this Christmas we will be spared everyone else's traumas and frustration. It will just be the three of us.

You must make a point of seeing old Nannie when you come home. She is longing to see you and hear your news.

I still have not had any word from Cardiology. I hope it will be early in 1989. I get awfully tired nowadays.

I am longing to get all your news. There never seems to be time to hear it all. Hope you don't find Edinburgh too dull.

Take care.

Love and kisses,

From Mumsie xxx

15 December 1988

My Dearest Wee Girl,

Looking forward to seeing you in a week's time. We will have a good time, you will see.

I enclose a thank-you letter for Jim once more. I am a wonderful mum you know. I can't sit your exams in June (I am no good at them). Think you will manage without

Mumsie? You manage to spend the cash without Mumsie's help but oh dear, poor wee girlie can't write thank-you notes. Poor old Nannie was in tears today about the beautiful letter you didn't write her for her birthday fiver. It had pride of place on her sideboard and she made me sit and read the letter I had written, while she wept at how sweet you were.

However, my love, I hope 1989 may bring a resolution to write your own. You have some very sweet sponsors, who are genuinely rooting for you and have faith in you (poor sods).

However, lectures over, back to mince and tatties, haggis and neeps, French toast, chicken, home-made soup, puddings and coconut cake under the bed, plus clean knickers, clean bras and showers – plus *Hannah and Her Sisters* every night in colour – a small compensation for the literary loss but I am longing to see you again and have news of the Capital City. You will have fun. It will be nice to see Alan and Anne and have the phone ringing at night again.

Enclosed, 2 Valium, which will render you unconscious.[7]
Love you,
Hugs and kisses,
Love in haste, Mumsie xxx

---

[7] After my initial disastrous overnight coach journey down to London when I was looking for accommodation, mum used to send me sleeping tablets she'd been prescribed to get me through subsequent trips.

1989, PART ONE

I Love You All Too, And Make Good Soup

It was good to see mum and dad again over the Christmas break and finally have positive things to tell them. Friends and family were invited over to the house during the festive season to hear all Laura's latest stories from the Big City. Having been apart from each other for a few months also meant I appreciated mum and dad so much more. Of course there were some blips, being back there after finally having been able to do my own thing, but it was generally a happy time. However, by the end of the break I was missing my new friends and looking forward to getting back down to London.

Over the course of the previous few months I'd made some great new pals from all over the UK and I loved the halls as there was always someone there to talk to at any given time of the day or night. Having a subsidised bar in the garden wasn't bad either. In mid-January I went to Amsterdam for a weekend with a group of the new friends I'd made. It was the first time I'd been on holiday with friends (apart from visiting Anne in Paris

33

just before I moved down to London). Although we had a great time, the combination of extremely powerful cannabis and my shock at witnessing decriminalised prostitution for the first time soon threw me into a huge, prolonged panic attack which eventually led to us having to return to London early.

Having always lived in Scotland prior to going to polytechnic, I had grown up with the usual Scottish chip on my shoulder that people who lived in London and the south of England were evil oppressors. I expected a lot of hostility from English people but experienced none in all my time down there. On the contrary, people seemed glad to have a 'token Jock' as a friend.

Thursday, 19 January 1989

My Dearest Laura,

Seeing as you were complaining that I had not written for weeks and I was touched that you appreciated my 'pearls of wisdom' and considering that in the mountain of stationery there was a reasonably nice pack of 'Waverley' notelets still *virgo intacto*, here I am again.

I thought you would like to know just as I started this letter, the late unlamented Andy Pandy of dubious alcoholic reputation, the cause of so much unhappiness and misunderstanding in the past, forgetful of the fact that on the last occasion I had referred to him as 'an odious little toad' or 'obnoxious little scab' or some other term of endearment, phoned.[8] In his usual state of *delirium tremens*, unable to get a reply to the first Hird number he usually rings with his last 10p (Dad's sister-in-law – long deceased) was still left with his 10p to ring the 2nd number and ask with his usual eloquence, 'A wanny speak a' Aura.' You can appreciate the pleasure it gave me to inform 'the ragged-trousered philanthropist'[9] that you were in London (since September). His first 'oh' implied that you were in pursuit of things of the flesh but I advised him you were in pursuit of BA (Hons) in English Lit, had lots of intellectual friends and were doing extremely well.

'Things are no awfie guid the now, thatsh wy I thought ad gie Laura a ring. They might be better a morin,' he said. I said, 'good bye,' though thought 'good riddance' and said I would tell you he rang.

'Nuff about Andy. I am pleased your essays are nearly finished and you got good marks for your first two.

Work hard, Laura. Have some fun too but discipline yourself to work hard at all times. Those opportunities will not come again.

I ordered your trousers and they are sending them directly to you in the next few days. Send the advice note to me for payment right away. Hope you like them.

---

[8] The man I'd been having an on/off relationship with for three years prior to my move to London.

[9] Robert Tressell's novel about the lives of a group of painters and decorators which was Andy's favourite book and which he'd encouraged me to read.

I have not been doing anything exciting. I feel so tired these days. I see them at Cardio on 25th January.

I think my working days are numbered. I had to come home from work at 9.30 a.m. this morning because I could not breathe and slept until tea-time. It takes a real effort to get out at 8 a.m. and cope with a busy surgery. I am afraid housework is sometimes neglected. I look forward to the chance of maybe feeling like a whole person with some energy again. Hope it is not too long.

Sorry about writing. I still feel a bit dopey. I am looking forward to seeing your photos.

Uncle Jack is going into hospital tomorrow for a hernia operation. He always enjoys hospital because he gets a chance to rest and read and doesn't need to spend his day running around doing things for everyone – giving Margaret breakfast in bed, doing the shopping, running Jonathan to interviews. I don't know how they will cope without him for a couple of weeks. We should all take care of him more. He is in his 81st year and a very special man. I appreciate that. One of life's gents and a true friend.

Sorry this has not been one of the cheery specials. Try and get your cash sorted out before you spend any more.

I must have a wee rest now.

Hope to hear from you soon.

Love Mumsie XXX

P.S. Miss you but don't try to come home before Easter. Just make me proud of you.

28 January 1989

Saturday 11.45 p.m.

My Dearest Laura,

I loved your letter and loved your photos, particularly the
Peter Pan ones and the super one in your leather cap. I
would not mind a copy of that one. Ian thought you had
a real look of the Sixties. It was good to see your room
and your friends and to see you still managed your liquid
refreshments. Of course it was very gratifying to see the
legendary 'Bob a Job' at last. He looks very distinguished,
not a bit like I imagined but I liked him and Dad and I
thought your chums were sweet and look a lot of fun. I
hope you enjoyed the show the other night and had good
fun in Amsterdam. It is good being so near the Continent.
The coach trip from Edinburgh to Dover really puts one
off going. Thanks for the photos. I think they were super.
Of course Ian thought the instamatic 'gritty' but I thought
they were perfect, even the Peter Pan decapitation. Anyone
could take good photos with a £200 camera. Ian is just
back from Orlando. Like Morag, piles of snaps with Goofy,
Donald Duck, Mickey Mouse and Snow White and yup!
Sacrilege! One with 'Walt Disney's Peter Pan'. My Laura's
Peter Pan was the J.M. Barrie original from Kensington
Gardens where it all began. Disney's Tinker Bell had boobs
– uggh – JMB would turn in his grave.

I am so happy that your essays are finished and I can
stop moaning about that. I have now sent your cheque. I
can stop moaning about that too. And you sent me a lovely

letter as well. I love your letters. I read them over and over again. I have them all. I must have studied your photos a hundred times and wondered why everyone did not think them as wonderful as Dad and I did. Certainly I have not had a chance to show them to Margaret and Jack and Nannie and have not sent the Peter Pan one to Jim yet. They are all keen Laura fan-club members – people who see life through enchanted eyes.

We have not seen Margaret and Jack for a week, although I have been in constant contact by phone. Jack's routine operation has had complications because of his being on Warfarin and because of his heart condition. He is rather ill and only his family are allowed in for a short while each day. Dad and I visited him the day before the op and he was so full of fun, asking for you, sending his love. I was looking forward to showing him your photos and reading your letter to him. He has such faith in you.

I hope he makes it for his sake and Margaret's and selfishly because I am getting a bit short on lovely people who are tuned in to the same wavelength. There are more in the Never Never Land than here. Old Nannie complains about this. 'Apart from Dad, June and Laura, the lovely people have all gone.' She is not a very good judge of character where I am concerned but she did know some lovely people.

Enough of this depression. I am not sure if you know the poet, W.B. Yeats, an Irish revolutionary who wrote 'The Lake Isle of Innisfree'. I rediscovered one of his, which I loved, only a few days ago and I would like to share it with you, because he expresses so beautifully how I feel about you my beloved child and about the people I love. You should try and get a book about him from the library. You would love it.

He Wishes for the Cloths of Heaven

Had I the heavens' embroidered cloths
Enwrought with golden and silver light.
The blue and the dim and the dark cloths
Of night and light and the half-light
I would spread the cloths under your feet:
But I, being poor, have only my dreams;
I have spread my dreams under your feet;
Tread softly because you tread on my dreams.

After that I will retire to bed and finish this tomorrow, love.

Sunday 9 p.m.

Had a lazy day. Slept until 11a.m., did some washing and ironing. News of Jack no better, if anything a little worse. Our boarder, Colin, has gone, so we have no breakfasts to make. We did not make very much from him but after Christmas I had started putting away a fiver of his money each week for you as I had no 'Cloths of Heaven' to spread under your feet.

Unfortunately, he had this girlfriend who used to come and stay for days on end. We provided her with her food too and he never gave us any extra for her, she had baths, did her washing, stayed in all day when he was at work, burning all the lights, playing the TV. I had the gas central heating burning from 6a.m.–9a.m. and 4.30 until midnight full blast as they were always cold. I discovered by accident that they had been burning 2 bars of the electric fire all night and all day when she was in. As the meter wasn't locked she had been using the 10p you used all the time. I padlocked the meter and when they realised the game was up they left, owing me a week's rent.

I shudder to think what the next gas and electricity bills will be like. Naturally, I feel a bit sick about it all. He was a civil servant and I discovered he was being paid for his accommodation. I only took him as a favour to a friend. However, I am not going to make a fuss about it. Put it down to an expensive experience. I am still putting away my 1ps and twopences for your jar of coffee. Dad is glad he has gone. He always called him a 'dour wee bugger'.

Nikki is still slogging at university. She works in the library, doing homework until 9 p.m. and does homework all weekend. She has given up her job at Safeway. I hope you are working hard too. I am happy you have made so many new friends but you must remember to apply yourself to studies. They have to take priority.

Carole's bambino is still shaping up, although it poses a difficulty as to when the annual trip to Disneyland takes place this year but they are still going.

I will send your £40 off on Friday again.

I think old Jim may be sending you your fiver this week. If he does, I have enclosed the usual thank-you letter stamped. Hold on to it until he does and then get it off as soon as poss. Also, if you can send the typing he gave you, I will do it.

Your trousers should be with you by now. Ring and let me know if ok.

Have to get ready for work tomorrow.

Looking forward to hearing about Amsterdam.

Take care (or t'care).

Fondest love as ever and always,

Mumsie xxx

9 February 1989

My Dearest Wee Girl,

Surprise, surprise – 2 letters and a postcard from Amsterdam since you went home (sorry, I mean returned to London.) I always enjoy your letters. You make me feel ashamed of my poor literary output. I used to be such a prolific writer (another word for written diarrhoea) – a pen in my hand and there was no stopping me. I keep having ideas but can't get them on paper. Although a request for Scots poets (using broad Scots dialect) inspired the following, but don't worry. It was not presented for publication. I dried up but thought it would amuse you.

Oor Lass

Oor wee lassie's ga'en awa';
Ga'en awa' tae college.

> She ga'ed doon tae London toon
> Tae quench her drooth for knowledge.
> Wi' greetin' e'en oor wean left hame
> Ma hert wis unco' sair
> Fair trauchled doon wi books an' claes
> And a muckle teddy bear.

It is not quite Burns or Fergusson quality, but might be compared to Willie McGonagall on a bad day. Hugh MacDiarmid can rest in peace also.

Thought it would give you and your chums a giggle. I might have sent it off if I had ideas for more verses.

Wait a mo'. I feel one coming on:

> She ga'ed off tae Amsterdam
> Tae see the toon by nicht;
> But didnae ken the wee Dutch hoose
> Had a muckle big red licht.

I would have been better stifling that one, never mind. Rabbie must have had his off days too.

I am glad you are going to get down to work now. I was beginning to think you were quenching your drooth for knowledge with too much of our national beverages – McEwan's and Scotch. So work hard, my love. (I know Burns and Dylan Thomas were reputed to find inspiration in the bottom of a glass but they were already established by then and let's face it – they didn't live long – and just think of all the poems they could have written if they had lived another 10 or 20 years.)

Well, back to earth. Things are pretty much the same. Still puffing and blowing like a geriatric going to work but 2 squirts of Ventolin and a couple of deep breaths in the common room and the patients hardly guess I am ready for the knacker's yard. Although occasionally one meets the odd perceptive one who says, 'You sound worse than I feel.' Never mind. I am a tough old nut like my mum was.

Jack is still in hospital. 3 weeks for an op that should have taken 5 days. Dad and I visited on Saturday and he looked awful. Dad popped up to see Nannie on Sunday and she promised to burn a candle for him. When I returned on Monday he was improving gradually. Dear old Nannie. Dear old Jack – very special people. She is 90 in May and he is 81 in August. They think I am a wee lassie still, it's nice, so I hold on to them both and I love them both.

Not the way I love you (not the heavens' embroidered cloths way) but it is possible to love in so many different ways. In different heights and depths.

Alan has won a holiday to the Canary Islands, so he and Ian are going this year once they recover from the holiday in Florida and get back from their summer holiday in Bangkok and Singapore. I don't know how we found Paris and Austria so enchanting in comparison but we did. Happiness is where you find it and you don't need to look too hard.

Remember the lovely holidays we had in Blackpool with Grandma and Pappa? Going down to Uncle Peter's Variety Show at the Pavilion and on to the funfair and back to the boarding house for tea. Oh yes, *those* are holiday memories to treasure and we were happy – not very well off, but we were together.

Well, lass, it looks as if 'people are coming over' to visit at last – on Saturday – wish you were here. No excuse for not opening a few of those bottles at last. Sad you won't have the pleasure of a few wee drams before you top them up with water on Sunday. Just thought . . . you haven't? You didn't? You couldn't? Tell me the Drambuie isn't cold tea. No, you wouldn't. You couldn't. Just joking. Give us a ring on Saturday IF YOU DARE. Still joking, I think. I would love to hear from you. I can't send a wee dram on the phone or send a wee doggie bag but will miss you as always and ever.

It is nearly midnight and I am in a mood for writing for hours tonight but I must stop and post this to you.

Fondest love, hugs and kisses,

From Mumsie xxx

Wednesday, 15 February 1989

My Dearest Wee Girlie,

It was a freezing cold afternoon. Have been unable to leave the fire since I popped down to the bank to cash your £30 for Dad to send off tomorrow. Poor old Laura. The monthly sum becomes less and less, however, look on the bright side – if you have no money for distractions, there is nothing else to do but study – very character building and, boy, I am sure it will help with your exams. Sorry, wish I could be more help.

So as I was saying, it is cold. Did a competition for a holiday in Poland. (Want to come with me if I win?) Also did one for a night at the opera. *La Bohème, Don Giovanni* or *Das Rheingold.* Never have any luck with those. When I think of prizes I won when I was 35 coming up for 8 – happy days. The problem is I still have the mentality of a 10-year-old.

I am waiting for Dad coming home and Brian Tilsley snuffing it tonight on *Coronation Street* (really cultured stuff) so I thought I would write a wee note for my wee girl because she sounded wistful and sad the last 2 times she phoned. It might encourage her to write me another letter!!!!!!!

Remember the notepaper? (Designed by Andrex for a bulk order by Cash and Carry for a certain friend to use for birthday, Christmas and anniversary presents for the next 20 years.) Already I have an ottoman full of them.

Here's Dad – no it isn't – so I will keep on writing.

Well, the party was not the success I thought – too much food – chicken drumsticks, ham and broccoli and chicken and sweetcorn quiches, sausage rolls, savoury kievs, vol-au-vents, scotch eggs, salads plus raspberry pavlova, strawberry cheesecake, meringues and my usual home-baked sludge. The place was spotless. We even washed the wine glasses and washed the daddy-long-legs out of the light shades. I was exhausted doing such unusual tasks. I am sorry – there was not a single doctored bottle. Wish you had been there to take charge of the booze. Remember all those lovely bottles I have lovingly kept unopened for 'people coming over'? Well they came over and drank 8 bottles of wine, half a bottle of brandy, a bottle of whisky, $3/4$ a bottle of vodka and half a bottle of Cointreau and that was just 4 of them.[10]

Well, Dad's home, had tea, Brian Tilsley just bit the dust. We watched the *TV Times* Awards. I am sure it's a fix – Penelope Keith, Cliff, Cilla Black and Ian Holm won. French and Saunders and John Cleese did not have a look in.

So I decided to continue my letter. Sorry about the Valentine.[11] I nearly bought one twice but thought you would be annoyed at my lack of discretion. I got one as usual from old Jim. He always signs it in case I think someone else has sent it. Not many people send me Valentine's cards from Cambridge. He could have risked a 'Guess Who?' Dad gave me a toffee apple instead of a card – more practical. I should not criticise the Valentine donations to an old hag like myself, especially as I didn't send any.

Do let me know as soon as you get any more results. I am longing to hear.

Apart from the bar mitzvah on Saturday, life has been quiet, working hard, visiting Jack who has had 2 relapses.

---

[10] As mentioned before, mum had a tendency towards exaggeration sometimes.

[11] Mum used to send me a Valentine's card every year in which she tried to disguise her handwriting (or would get dad to write it) so I always received something on Valentine's Day.

He has been in hospital for 4 weeks and looks so thin and tired. I think it will be quite a while before we go 'jumbling' again. Do drop him a funny wee letter if you get any time. He would like that.

I visited old Nannie yesterday. She has been ill too. I went straight from work at 1.30 p.m. and got home at 7 p.m. with a cream cake, shortbread and tinned peaches stuffed in my bag. She is a wee darling. I took lunch for us both and she is always so pleased to see me, she tries everything to keep me there. She kept pouring me wine glasses full of 'cherry wine'. I sipped it slowly because it was strong but she just kept topping it up and saying, 'Drink up, pet.' She toasted her Laura 20 times and my operation 20 times, Laura's exams, Laura's graduation, Ronnie's job. When I stood up to wash the glasses I was p***** out of my mind. It had been cherry brandy – full strength – which she had brought back from Spain about 30 years ago. I couldn't see the bus numbers because all the Gorgie ones said 33333333 and then I changed buses at Haymarket for a 44444444 to Slateford Road. It was a good job it was a windy night. Everyone else was staggering so it didn't show. It seemed 5 miles from Slateford to the house. Nannie was planning her 90th birthday party on the 27th May and her funeral and asked me to take notes. She wants you to come to both but is going to try and postpone the latter until after your graduation. I hope she does. She is special.

I hope you are still enjoying yourself and working hard and washing your undies etc., etc.

I still miss you a bit but not so much knowing you are doing what you want.

This is not much of a letter. It was not an inspired one, an off the cuff one, and they are always boring, I am sure, but wanted you to have one for the weekend.

It won't be long until Easter. T'care. I love you.

Your loving Mumsie xxx & Dadsie xxx

Wednesday, 22 February 1989 – 3.40 p.m.

My Dearest Wee Girl,

I have just been to the bank to withdraw the cash for your weekly bread, so that Dad can transfer it to you tomorrow. Coming home I hit a freak storm, snow, hailstones, gales etc. It was awful, not even a St Bernard dog in sight, not even a drop of brandy in the house to revive me because our guests drank it all last weekend. So I compromised, a cup of hot coffee, a cosy fire to thaw out, feet up and I will at least make a start to reply to your super letter and photos received today. My, that trip to Amsterdam was more traumatic than the *Canterbury Tales*, Johnson's tour of Scotland and the *Pilgrim's Progress* all rolled into one. (Can I keep the photos a few more days?)

You needn't worry about going to Poland (if I won, ha). It is a Catholic country and sin is not as much a way of life as it is in Presbyterian countries. We found this also about Austria. Everything was so wholesome and clean and decent. I know you will say, 'What about Paris?' and Madame Fifi and her sex shop and Pigalle, but they were so friendly about it. You will now say, 'What about our friend – the spear-throwing Rambo in the Metro?'[12] – well he was just a sweet, heroin-addicted schizo guy who didn't like having his photo taken.

I am on to the yellow paper today. Cam is really a sweet person giving us a ton of multi-coloured notepaper. I think it was for our health's sake, rather than her pocket's sake. She is retiring later this year and ending my lucrative little sideline – boarders boo hoo. I will have to think of something else like writing my memoirs!!

Sorry I was side-tracked. Why is it healthy to write on technicoloured notepaper? – well according to a TV programme last week bleached paper contains the deadly poison dioxin. Tea bags, coffee filter paper, white tissues and toilet paper, disposable nappies and tampons, and notepapers are all suspect. Only recycled paper is safe.

* N.B. A healthy pink one [*A new sheet of pink notepaper.*]

Who wants to write a letter on a recycled tampon, toilet roll or nappy? Even if one does tend to write a lot of verbal diarrhoea, one doesn't need to have one's nose rubbed in it as a punishment. Thought-provoking isn't it?

---

[12] During a holiday to Paris with mum and dad a couple of years before I moved down to London we had been mugged in the Metro after I took a photo of a vagrant who was carrying a spear. He ran across to our platform, prodded me with the spear until I handed over the camera, jumped on it and kicked it onto the line.

Talking about writing, could you remember to send me old Jim's thingy he wants typed. He phones every week to ask me if you have typed it and every month to ask about your fiver. Drives me bonkers.

I loved your photos. Pleased to see you are getting a lot of wear from your new hat and gloves but darling you don't need to wear them in bed. I loved the one with the chap with the dummy and teddy bears. Hope he doesn't wear Pampers. He could be doing his health a lot of harm. I am glad you didn't take your teddy to Amsterdam with you. He led a very sheltered life in Edinburgh, even wearing blinkers when you were naughty. I wouldn't want him to mix with Dutch bears. I went around with a Dutch boor, so I know what I am talking about. Just expose dear Ted to the 'bear necessities of life'. Remember Sebastian's poor bear in *Brideshead Revisited*. University life was too much for him – and don't take him to Paddington to meet that poofy bear in the wellies and raincoat.

Poor Carole has had food-poisoning from a tuna-fish sandwich she bought from Crawford's. Poor soul she had 3 days of purging and couldn't even keep water down. Auntie reported it to the Public Health. Heaven help Crawford's. Her 4-month pregnancy has been rather nasty so far. She didn't need this. Did Anne know she was pregnant? Tell Anne.

Don't waste your precious money on me for Mother's Day. I will ask you for hand-outs all the time when you are rich and famous. One of your special . . .

[*Letter carries over onto blue notepaper with 'N.B. A healthy blue one now — recycled Andrex!!'*]

. . . home-made cards will be treasured greatly and I will love it just as much. It is the thought that counts, not the value.

Anyway I am thinking of the nice little retirement cottage (with the slightly bigger memory garden and no man-eating rose bush to attack people when they try to visit) that you will insist on buying us when your first novel sells its 10 millionth copy. Well if Jackie Collins can do it with no brains, it will be easy for my baby with 2 'ologies' in her passes. I was so pleased to hear that all your essays had passed. Now for As and Bs in the exams!!! What a pushy mother.

Do you realise you horrid child it is 5.30 p.m. My coffee's cold. Dad will be rushing home to see how Brian Tilsley's funeral is progressing on *Coronation Street* and no tea ready. Just because you say write soon and you know my weakness when I pick up a pen and recycled whatever, I can't stop. I can remember when you were small and didn't want to sleep (which was often) you would say, 'Read me another poem, Mummy.' Like 'No Telephones in Heaven'. (Wouldn't it be nice if there were telephones in Heaven. I would never be off the phone – I know lots of lovely people there.) – Well, where was I? Yes, sometimes you would say, *The Pied Piper of Hamelin*, knowing I love reading poetry aloud as much as I like writing. I can remember another night a few weeks ago when you said, 'Do you want to hear my favourite tapes and we will reminisce and drink gin and martini cocktails.' We cried and laughed and talked until 3.30 a.m. and Dad raged and talked about going to bed – it was lovely – you know I love listening to music nostalgically and a bit tiddly. 'Hush-A-Bye Mountain.' I will always remember that night.

It is a wise child who recognises her mother's weaknesses. You realise I will tell those stories on *This is Your Life, Laura Hird* and they won't even have time for the commercials because talking about you is another one of my weaknesses.

It is now 6 p.m. – place like a midden heap. Now June, be calm, 2 macaroni cheeses out of the freezer. Pop in the oven, some frozen chips and a choc-ice and say 'Ron, I had such a tiring day at surgery, haven't been able to get off my bum since I came home.' Quick alibis – another weakness. Have fun with Anne. Give her my love. T'care both of youse.

Love you.

Lots of hugs and kisses,

Your Mumsie xxx

Tuesday, 9 March 1989

My Dearest Laura,

I was delighted to receive your very unusual Mother's Day present, card and delightful Jelly Baby packing. Yum yum. A week on Friday until you return home I must hurry with my *Clochemerle* memoirs so that you can read it and then

I must start to gut the boxroom just in case the sitting room is occupied – hope not – but might be. But trying to save up for a little holiday before the op.

I loved your card, not the kind I could show anyone but typically Laura and everyone else's mother gets mushy cards but I am not everyone else's mum – I am Laura's.

I am enclosing 2 sleeping tablets for the journey to Edinburgh. The last 2 (those are sleeping tablets same as the first ones I sent you). Thursday, Dad will pay your last £30 to the bank plus your return fare, which I have made up to £20, so that will be £50.

I feel rather sad today. Old Nannie had a fall yesterday and fractured her femur. She fell at 9 a.m. in the morning. The warden at the flat put her in a chair and did not return until 5 p.m. She had been unable to get out of the chair.

Audrey did not phone me until 3 p.m. today. She had not seen Nannie since New Year's Day. Dad and I went to see her on Saturday for Mother's Day. (I saw a nice card – 'To Nannie on Mother's Day'.) We got some grapes for her. She was rushing to get to church to burn her candles and say her masses for everyone, so Dad and I took her there on the bus and saw her safely in church.

Poor wee Nannie was planning her 90th birthday party – 3-course dinner with 40 guests, a band and entertainers. I promised to return this week to help her write the invitations. She had her favourite model dress, which I bought for her at a jumble sale, cleaned. It was a lovely dress and she looked super in it. It was a Paris model, size 14 – only cost me a quid and she loved it.

I am not sure if she will survive this. She is 89 and will be operated on today or tomorrow. She is such a frail little sparrow but quite unique. I have loved her since I was a little baby. She bought me my only teddy. Say a little prayer for her if you can. She has kept us all safe, burning her candles and no-one burns them for her.

Nannie always used to ask me to compile a will for her so that Audrey, as next of kin, would not get the lot. I always told her she would live forever. I couldn't bear to arrange a will for her.

Now I am not sure what to do. Dad and I got the chance of a cheap holiday – 8 days in Yugoslavia, before the op. I feel so tired – it would buck me up. Half board, flying from Glasgow to Pula. It would cost over £100 to fly to London. It would cost more for a week's stay at Crieff.[13] The doctor said it would be ok if I fly. It is travelling long distances by bus or train which would be dangerous for circulation to the heart. 2 hours on a plane is ok.

We had quite made up our minds to go ahead last night but now I am not sure. If anything happened to Nannie when I was away I would never forgive myself.

I am looking forward to seeing you. Sorry if I have waffled on about Nannie but I just feel she cared about

---

[13] When I was young we spent a few holidays at Crieff Hydro, a hotel in Perthshire which at the time was run by the Church of Scotland and unlicensed. This made sneaking a bottle of Pimm's in to drink in the hotel room when Margaret and Jack came to visit all the more fun!

everyone and nobody cared about her. Everyone asks me to tell her they will see her soon but they never do. She wasn't invited back after struggling to Pappa and Grandma's funerals. I was probably the only one left who cared and I could have cared a lot more.

Sorry I am going on again. If you get a chance to bring home some things you don't need, do so at Easter – it will save you in the summer, because you will never get all that stuff home in the summer.

This might be the last letter before I see you. I look forward to my girl being home again.

Sorry it is such a miserable letter. Not my usual.

Fondest love, hugs and kisses as always,

From your Mumsie xxxx

The lodger, Colin, had returned briefly when I was home for the Easter break, but it was good to be back in the 'boxroom' and I had fun catching up with my friends, going to the cinema, cooking for and watching videos with mum and dad and a lovely night of nattering and (more) gin with mum. After going back to London following the break, I met and began a relationship with David, a philosophy student who was due to graduate the following term. Mum was delighted that I'd finally met someone my own age, as my previous relationships up to this point had all been with men old enough to be my father or grandfather. I used to say that this was because when I was young, rather than take me to see

Disney and kids' films at the cinema, mum would take me to see the films she liked herself – romantic comedies and musicals where the male and female leads were invariably decades apart.

Wednesday, 12 April 1989

My Dearest Wee Girl,
I have been picking up discarded packets of baccy and enclose them in the hope that they will tide you over until the duty-free bonanza. I have ordered your jogging pants but there is a 2 to 4 week delay, so try not to bend for a month. They will be coming directly.

The house seems strangely quiet and yet I miss you already. 'These foolish things remind me of you,' as the lyricist says. Walking ankle-deep through a field of last week's used knickers, stubbing one's toe on a mountain of empty beer cans or rolling on an empty wine bottle concealed in a poly bag carried home the night before as part of your anti-rape and -mugging campaign.

It is so sweet. Neighbours are stopping me in the street and saying, 'I hear Laura has gone back to London.'

I am just saying this to hide my breaking heart, as I nostalgically remember the evening meals you made and the night we drank the bottle of gin and martini and watched Jack Nicholson on video, doctoring Dad's drink with cola and yet he had to go to bed, stoned, drinking half what we had.

I remember fondly the shopping trips we almost made together – things like that are important to mothers. The best-laid schemes of mice and men ebbing away as you continued to lie in bed like a beached whale as the morning hours trickled away.

Sad, I could be very poor the next time you come home and maybe will never be able to afford to shop with you again. After Orca, my 'dour wee bugger', finally left for good, I was at a loose end between work, getting ready for hols, and answering Cam's mail and phone. So I have signed on to help Jim Sillars and the Scottish Nationalist Party fight the poll tax. We refuse to pay, even if we are incarcerated, castrated and crucified. 'We arra people.' 'Scotland the Brave.' 'Up yer kilt' and all that. I feel like a Covenanter or a Flora MacDonald.

How was the vegetarian haggis? You could not give Burns' 'Ode to a Haggis' because he refers to paunch, tripe or thairm – unless you used verse 5.

> Is there that owre his French ragout
> Or olio that wad staw a sow
> Or fricassee wad make her spew
> Wi perfect sconner.

Oh, shut up, June. Was it good?

Hi, your latest batch of photos arrived. I have enclosed them. More memories of Amsterdam??

Well, we are only 2½ days away from our holiday. Still washing and ironing constantly and still that ironing never gets any less. Some time when you are home I will challenge you to empty the ironing basket for the first time in years. I will tell you there's a fiver hidden in one of the shirt pockets!!!

Dad has packed a pair of shorts – he looks like a very fat Alec Guinness coming off the *Bridge Over the River Kwai*. He has packed his swimming trunks too – he will be like father of Orca – varicose veins and pot belly. Ha, I should talk. I am taking Auntie's bikini. Yugoslavia here we come. I will miss hearing your news for a week. Ring me on the Saturday night we come home – 22nd April. I will give you all the news. If you are writing to thank Jim for the £5 (if he sends it), don't mention we are in Yugoslavia because I always say I am too frail to go to Cambridge!!

Ian and Alan are running us through to Glasgow on Saturday morning for the flight. I am looking forward to flying – first time in 20 years. I am not scared at all – but our will and insurance policies are on top of the big wardrobe in a black briefcase. The bank books are in the brown briefcase in Dad's wardrobe and the gold rings are locked in a suitcase in my music box on my little wardrobe and you can have my *Peter Pan and Wendy* book and *Complete Works of J.M. Barrie*.

Don't spend it all on booze and roll-ups. Oh well, I have really scared myself now. I will have to do a Margaret and get drunk and be carried on board. She's terrified of flying.

I am watching a quiz programme – why don't you go on and make some cash. The competitors are dim.

Schubert wrote the *Jupiter Symphony*. In which G&S opera did Poo Bah appear – *Madame Butterfly*. Rubella is another name for mumps. Orpheus was the winged horse in Greek mythology. The Carrington family appear in *EastEnders*. My dear girl, you are *Mastermind* material. Specialised subject – Charles Bukowski, Woody Allen or Dennis Nilsen.[14] The general knowledge is a cakewalk as we know. We usually get 7 on the whole show. Have you settled down now? I hope so. I know you will be suffering withdrawal symptoms from my tomatie soup with chunks of ham, chicken broth with chunks of chicken and tattie soup with chunks of beef. Never mind. You will have them again.

We are missing the 'dour wee bugger's' money but never mind. I will find some other way of saving pennies for your coffee jar.

The *News* still haven't published my memoirs. They just don't recognise my true literary genius. I think I will try *The Beano* or *The Dandy*. The *Reader's Digest* didn't publish a story, either. I know it was only because I returned the key of the Porsche they kept offering me. Neither Dad nor I could drive – it seemed a waste. Still, they might have published my story. It would have been cheaper.

It is sickening all the agencies have been advertising

---

[14] I corresponded with serial killer Dennis Nilsen for several months for a paper I was writing for the course on books and dramatisations based on real-life murder cases.

for temps this week and today the sun shone and my little girl has gone.

Oh my love, I simply must finish now. I still have heaps to do. I still think you should have your grant sent weekly as before.[15] You know what you are like.

I am sending a longer letter so that you can read a paragraph a day and not miss hearing from me for ages.

I will tell you about all the trials and tribulations of our holiday in my next letter. Will send a postcard too – wow-eeh.

Until then, work <u>very hard</u>, write originally, remember James Michener and how he helped Rodgers and Hammerstein[16] and remember if Maria Von Trapp had become a nun, she couldn't have helped them either.

Also, if you go for a Saturday job, wear a dress for the interview – no baggy pants, greasy jumper, leather hat and gloves with missing fingers and leave your Doc Martens. Please Laura, just for Mumsie.

I am definitely going. I am making the kedgeree you didn't want and I know Dad is going to say, 'it's awfie dry'. There's no pleasing some folk. I am going to make scrambled eggs or Scotch pies for every meal – less work and it is as well too – have less complaints when you don't put any effort into it.

---

[15] My first term at polytechnic, when I received my grant I sent it to mum and she used to send it to me in weekly instalments.
[16] The musical *South Pacific* was based on Michener's *Tales from the South Pacific*.

Say 'hi' to anyone who may be reading this. I love you all too, and make good soup. Hope to meet you sometime.

Love and kisses.

Miss you

Mumsie xxxx

Sunday, 23 April 1989

My Dearest Wee Girl,

Well here we are at home after a week in a truly amazing country of differing provinces, differing climates, differing religions, some parts in extreme poverty, others extremely wealthy. The one thing they all have in common is loyalty to the Communist Party – and a reverent, adoring worship of their late leader Marshal Tito. His photo is in every shop, market, hotel, bank and public building. He was their leader during the Second World War and after and has been dead for many years. The country is crippled by inflation which benefits the tourists but destroys the country's economy. Still, enough about economies.

We did enjoy our impromptu holiday. It was a beautiful luxury hotel. Our first-floor room had a balcony which overlooked the bay. It was so soothing being lulled to sleep by the lapping of the waves against the rocks. Dad was drooling over the huge breakfasts. No limit to what one was allowed to eat and as you know there is no limit to Dad's appetite.

I will be writing a much fuller description of our holiday in a few days. I am a bit tired but wanted your baccy and lighter to reach you. I have not smoked for a week and that is something with 200 duty-frees in my case.

I think you will be able to use the other contribution. [*A box of tampons.*]

I thought you sounded a bit pensive last night. Hope all is well with you. Write and let me know if all is well. Or if all is not we can always work out something if we put our heads together.

I missed you last week and wished I was sharing it all with you.

Take care my love.

Fondest love,

From Mumsie

Monday, 24 April 1989 – in bed

My Dearest Laura,

Dr H has just gone – hoped he wouldn't need to come back and I could get out and have a pub lunch, have a run with Margaret and Jack and visit old Nannie, get the ironing up to date!!! I had even contemplated a cheapy midweek return to London as I am still on holiday but no – he is coming back on Thursday and sending a physio-therapist to pummel the fluid off my lungs every morning – a fair scunner – the dour wee bugger. The fluid on the lungs is a build-up of Yugoslavian wine I am sure. Don't worry I am 'no bad', still have a sense of fun and no temperature and no ankle swelling – just one of those nasty colds one gets with a change of air. I missed the pollution and nicotine, have given up fags and didn't know the Yugoslav word for antibiotics.

Dad has been his usual tower of strength. I have already had a plate of soup on a mucky tray spilled over my nightie and a cup of wishy-washy tea (lukewarm – thank God) over my chest. When we run out of the Capital Meat Centre's macaroni & cheese, lasagne and taglia-thingy we will be starving. He had a traumatic day yesterday; Sunday. I am in the sitting room (my wee girl's room); when I shut my eyes I can hear my Laura playing the piano and Alan on the flute, it keeps me company when I am on my own.

So back to Dad's trauma. He came through saying there were no goodies, boo hoo. I baked a tin of oat crunchies (new recipe) before we went on holiday. 'I have eaten them all – boo hoo,' he cried, 'and all my socks are smelly.' Hadn't been washed for 2 weeks, no wonder. 'How can I wash socks and bake goodies when I am confined to bed?' I asked. 'Don't know how you are going to manage it,' he said. The smelly socks are still in the Ali Baba[17] on Monday, that's why I am sleeping in the sitting-room. When you open the bedroom door you get the 'Humming Chorus' from *Madame Butterfly* from the Ali Baba. This is only a rehearsal. I don't think the house will be standing when I return after the op – he tries but he is just so used to me doing everything.

Enough about my cold and incidents – you must be dying to hear about the holiday.

---

[17] A wicker laundry basket

It was a lovely plane – not a Pan Am jumbo but any plane seems lovely if you haven't flown since the Wright brothers and Amy Johnston. I was a wee bit concerned about the Captain taking a walk down the aisle and asking if we were enjoying ourselves. I wanted to say, 'Should you no be back in your cabin, Captain, in case we hit a mountain, Jimmy?'

We had a meal and half a bottle of wine each free. The other booze had to be paid for – only 60p. When she asked Dad if he wanted whisky, gin, vodka, rum or brandy he asked for another half-bottle of the free wine and got it – I could have thumped him. He was the only passenger who had his safety-belt on for the full flight and spent a good bit of the journey reading instructions on 'How to inflate your dinghy'.

There were mostly people from Edinburgh on board and some real toughies from Glasgow, wearing straw hats in the rain at Glasgow airport and their canvas shoes were sopping by the time they got on board. They filled their bladders for the first half of the journey and emptied them for the second half, singing all the time, 'A belong tae Glesga', 'Sshcotland the Brave', 'There wis a sodger – a Sco'ish sodger' – oh boy, were they sloshed.

As I have said the hotel was beautiful and the food very plentiful, in fact Dad could have sat and ate from 7 a.m. until 9 a.m. and no-one would have said 'Stop'. He tried his best – sausages, scrambled eggs, ham omelettes, 4 cheeses, 4 cold meats, 4 jams, 6 rolls and Vienna bread and all washed down with gallons of coffee.

It was 'boo hoo' if we had to leave the table when there was still food left. He must be finding a difference this week.

Pula itself was a beautiful town, with a huge Roman amphitheatre in the centre – perfectly preserved by the mild weather. It looked exactly as it was in the days when Peter Ustinov fed Richard Burton to the lions.

The Yugoslavs all do National Service and the Naval Academy is in Pula. The town is full of tall, handsome young soldiers. Alan would have been overjoyed at the sight. The girls are all very plain.

Well love, since I last wrote Auntie Morag called with some soup for tomorrow's lunch and then Margaret and Jack called with some Roundas for our tea. It is nice to have friends when you're 'no weel', rather like a friendly 'meals on wheels' service.

Now where was I – yes on Tuesday we had our greatest adventure – a full-day trip to Venice. That was something. We started off at 7 a.m. and returned back to the hotel at half an hour after midnight. It was wonderful, St Mark's Square, the Bell Tower, the Doge's Palace, the Bridge of Sighs, the Rialto Bridge and those chappies in the gondolas looking as if they were waiting for a Cornetto or a part in *The Gondoliers.* Dad has finally got his Cannellonis and Canalettos sorted out after seeing the actual scenes from the paintings, ah yes, travel broadens the mind.

We saw the church where Vivaldi was organist, the house of the chap who wrote *Death in Venice* and another one of Ernest Hemingway's favourite cafés. He certainly got around, didn't he? I don't know how he had time to write, the time he spent in cafés all over the world. I kept expecting to see Dirk Bogarde, with wee dyed moustache or Donald Sutherland chasing little dwarfs in red macs. In fact, actual death in Venice is a problem. We passed the local undertakers – two black-draped gondolas intact with coffins and flowers. The mind boggled – a Catholic country and no ground in which to bury – only water – but we discovered there was an island for that purpose, a sort of Père La'goon Chaise!!! Pardon the pun, I don't like sick jokes but couldn't resist making that one up. We went for a water-bus run around all the islands in Venice. It was super; a motor boat. Of course the Glaswegians were shouting, 'Fur Goad's sake shut the bus windae a'm droonin.' Venice is an experience, just as Paris was and Vienna, more treasures for the memory bank. I wish I had started travelling when I was still reasonably fit, however I always did enjoy doing things the hard way.

We went to a village party on Thursday – free booze and meal. It started at 7 p.m., welcome of local liqueurs, bread & onion. It tasted like surgical spirit and burned your throat. Inside, 8 to a table – 8 litres of wine to a table, every time a bottle was empty it was refilled, lots of local dancing and singing. We danced, we sang, we drank. They didn't serve the food until 10.30 p.m. We were all 'nissed as pewts' by then. Oh what a hangover. I remember the last time I felt like that I was trying to remember the words of a song – what was it again? You kept saying, 'Drink lots of water, Mum.'

Well it's now 8.30 p.m. Dad just made the Roundas, uggh – frozen mince centres – half-cooked greasy chips, no salt. You would think something would have been edible. Gosh I'm hungry – I am going to let him get pies tomorrow. You can't spoil a pie unless you burn it!! At least I saw *Coronation Street*. Didn't have it in Yugoslavia.

Remember the competition I did on the American Civil War? I won a miniature of Southern Comfort and a tape – I am enclosing the tape for you, plus your other goodies. Hope you like them.

The trousers came back – wish I could get you others. How are the shoes bearing up?

I hope all is well with you and you are working hard. It won't be long until exam-time now.

Do send me a letter sometime and tell me how life is in London.

I have been writing this off and on for 10 hours, what a blether.

Miss you, love you little girl.

Fondest loving kisses,

From Mumsie xxx

Thursday, 27 April 1989

My Dearest Wee Girl,

I am waiting for your favourite doctor to call and the physios and while I was waiting Auntie called and brought in your letter and cheque and I said you were having trouble with the phones and I couldn't ring you back and she suggested going down to the post office for me and getting you £2 worth of phone cards to phone people and I thought that was a good idea and she got the phone cards and here they are and now I want to post them to reach you for the weekend and you can phone Anne and me and whoever you want. Could only get £1 ones but you just use wee bits of them the man said (now wouldn't James Joyce have been proud of that sentence and you think you have problems with paragraphing).

You seem to have an awful lot to do poor Laura but it will be challenging. I will keep my fingers crossed and pray for your exams and return your lucky horseshoe in the meantime.[18] Your need is greater than mine. You can always return it for the operation.

I will attend to your cheque as usual.

Auntie has been providing me with lunch every day, which is very kind as I am only allowed up to the loo and it never occurs to Dad that I might get hungry between 10.30 a.m. when he leaves and 7.30 p.m. when he returns and seems amazed that the evening meal does not cook itself and dirty socks and shirts stay in the basket if you don't wash them and freezers and goody tins do not replenish themselves like the 'horn of plenty'.

---

[18] Small plastic lucky horseshoe which mum and I used to exchange, depending on who was needing luck most at any given time.

He still floats through 'wraith-like' in the evening like the ghost of Jacob Marley. 'My goody-box is empty – woe is me, woe is me.'

Auntie gave me a few oat crunchies and Melting Moments and I am doing a 'Ronnie' keeping them hidden under the bed.

I will give him choccie biccies for his birthday tomorrow. I have sent him a nice card and a wee present from you. I don't have a present for him. First time ever but I will get him something later.

The doc & physios have been. I am not allowed back to work on Monday – that's a nuisance, isn't it?

Carole's maybe coming over for a wee while this afternoon. She has only about 8 weeks to go. If she has a wee girl she is thinking of calling her Lauren. It would be nice to have a Laura & a Lauren in the family.

Ian goes off to Bangkok next Wednesday for 2 and a half weeks. I shall miss him. I know he gets on my nerves sometimes but it's only because he's my wee brother and I love him (and my gouty knees don't help sometimes!). He ran us through to Glasgow for the flight and came to meet us when we returned which was nice.

I am much better today – my suntan is back and my peely-wally look is going.

Miss you – kiss you,

Mumsie xxx

23 May 1989

My Dearest Laura,

Just a quick note enclosing another application form for work in the summer. It seems very good, although preference will be given to law students, but not absolutely necessary. You can tell them you did cataloguing for Rae Macintosh, and have typed reports. The wage isn't bad and you would be better off with a permanent summer job than waiting for the agencies.

I have filled in your NI number. Don't forget to send a covering letter, marked for the attention of the Personnel Manager.

I hope all is well with your essays and exam work and you are not finding this hot weather too unbearable. Dad got his arm badly burned by the sun on Sunday.

If you have time, drop me a wee note and let me know what plans you have made for next term (all going well) and what about your luggage? I feel a bit anxious.

I have to make this short so that I can get this off to you. They want the application in soon.

Perhaps you should ask them to send any correspondence here or phone here. It might save time. I can ring you at college if anything transpires. Hope you managed to get the others off.

Must dash now.

Fondest love,

Mumsie xxx

[*Uncompleted application form still in envelope with stamped addressed envelope − unused.*]

June (exam time) 1989

Thursday evening

My Dearest Laura,
Sorry I have been so lazy about writing this term. Not that I don't love writing to you as the prolific, literary beast which wended its way to you first and second terms would bear witness, but I seem to get so tired after a morning's surgery. Coping with the flotsam and jetsam of humanity, trying to sort out the hypochondriacs from the genuine cases in an overworked National Health Service, which is about to be demolished by Maggie T. and company.

However, I do not want to start my first letter in ages on the depressing subject of Maggie the witch.

I was so happy to receive your very welcome long letter and to once again visualise a composite picture of your life in London over the past few weeks. So much more satisfying than those phone calls – 'Hello mum, how are you?' 'I am fine – bloody hot' – peep, peep, peep – 'Phone in a couple of days.' Not that I do not love any call, no matter how short.

I would love to meet David. I like him already. He sounds really sweet and we are so happy you are going to share a flat next term with someone who is kind and caring and the fact that you are both interested in the same things seems wonderful. Now all you have to do is pass those exams and you can look forward to starting your second year. Are you still going to Enfield?[19]

I shall be rooting for you on Tuesday and Wednesday. I shall be sending vibrations all day, both days. Please phone me as soon after 6 p.m. as you can. I shall be like a wrung-out chamois. I am sure you will be the same but I know you will pull out all the stops at the last minute. What was wrong with *Little Dorrit* anyway? At least it was safe. I can understand. I wanted to do *Under Milk Wood* or *Hamlet* when *Death of a Salesman* was decided upon and 'Tam o' Shanter' and *A Shropshire Lad* instead of boring Ted Hughes.[20] However, sometimes it is easier to give in to safe and boring than follow the challenge which may be beyond one's capabilities. It is too late now, so go ahead and do your best. Examiners sometimes admire one for accepting a challenge but you need to know your subject.

I think Margaret's advice to have a hearty breakfast and get some glucose sweets for energy on the day was good. I think we will get a medical check-up for you when you come home plus a dentist and optician, some beef steaks, liver, haggis, fresh veg and fruit too.

---

[19] My first year at Middlesex Polytechnic was based at the All Saints campus in Tottenham. The second year was based in Ponders End, Enfield.

[20] Mum studied for Higher English in an evening class from 1985 to 1986. Unfortunately she became ill just prior to the exam so did not get a certificate in the end.

We are having a picnic with Margaret and Jack tomorrow. The wind is howling and hailstones battering down, so here's hoping the weather improves.

Nannie's party was a great success.[21] She looked stunning in a jade-green dress, with jade earrings and her hair perfect. The dress was a Paris model I bought for her in a charity shop in Galashiels. Cost me £1. Everyone asked where she got it. 'June bought it for me,' she said truthfully. Mandy H's mum is warden at the sheltered housing where Nannie stays. She played the piano all evening. Mandy and her 2 sisters were there (remember they used to sing in Princes Street Gardens?). They are good.

There was a compère and a male singer. Everyone did their party pieces. Nannie sang beautifully 'The Eriskay Love Lilt' and 'Coming Through the Rye'. She was fantastic. Audrey warned me that Nannie wanted to recite a tragic poem I used to recite when I was 12. Did I ever recite it to you? About 2 little orphan boys who lived in a rat-infested attic. The youngest boy, Jamie, is dying of hunger and the older boy steals a pie to save him from death and is arrested (a touch of *Les Misérables* – and boy was it miserable!) I had no copy of the poem as we couldn't afford books when I was young but I discovered that 40-odd years later, I could remember it all apart from a few lines. I tried to persuade Nannie not to ask for my recitation of 'A God After All' but no, her mind was made

---

[21] Nannie's 90th birthday party.

73

up. It was bl**** awful in front of 40 people, this depressing poem. I would rather have sang 'White Wings' and cried.[22]

It was hardly a howling success. The 80-year-olds were saying, 'Speak up hen, ma hearin' aid's oan the blink.' After this slow handclap, I went over to Nannie. 'You missed a couple of lines,' said she. Oh well, *c'est la vie*, the harder you try to please people!!! Dad, Ian and Alan refused to do party pieces, feigning lack of talent and she kissed <u>them</u> all goodnight!!!

There was a super buffet – half a bottle of whisky, a bottle of sherry and half a bottle of vodka and 6 cans of beer – and we had a super time, knowing old Nannie was happy on her 90th birthday. Afterwards, I asked Ian and Alan in for a bottle of chilled Riesling and it fell out of the fridge and smashed. I had just said, 'Come in and we will crack open a bottle of wine before you go home.' You should have seen Ian's face.

Well, darling, it is 11.30 p.m. and I have a Saturday surgery with 'my favourite doctor'! so I have to get my beauty sleep and sharpen my wits to be a step ahead of him. If Maggie T. knew about him she would make him Minister of Health.

Dad sends his love and best wishes for your exams, as do Ian, Alan, Margaret, Jack, Cam, Jim, Nannie and

---

[22] 'White Wings' was a song written by Banks Winter in 1912 and was a favourite of my mother's beloved granny. Mum would often dig out the sheet music at family parties, play it on the nearest piano, sing along and cry for her granny.

Uncle Tom Cobley and all[23] and you know how much love and best wishes mumsie sends you. I enclose 3 new pens for good writing, the lucky horseshoe again for good luck and £5 for a good breakfast before the exams.

Lots and lots of love and good wishes for good luck, good health and happiness in all you do, my love.

A big hug to David. Looking forward to meeting him.

Still miss you,

Love & kisses from Mumsie xxxx

June 1989

Dear Laura,

These are the blouses I bought for you today. They are nice and fresh and cotton and polyester and viscose which should wash well by hand but might need a wee iron. They should look nice with your new cardi and velvet skirt or over your trousers. They will be cool enough on their own during the summer and autumn.

Hope you don't mind the logo on the pocket of the striped one but it will not be seen under your cardi. The 22 is a big fit and measured 46". The 24 is very roomy and it is the dearer one. If you don't like either or both just post them back to me. I have the receipt and can exchange them or take them back. Don't wash your

---

[23] Whimsical English language expression taken from the Devon folk song, 'Widecombe Fair'. 'Old Uncle Tom Cobley and all' basically means 'et cetera'.

blouses with the other washing. Wash by hand and hang up to drip dry.

Hope you like them. You could do with something bright and fresh.

What do you think of your old Mum winning a £100 dinner at the Caledonian Hotel.[24] Wow eck, won't this make up for no-one asking me out at Christmas and New Year. Will give you all the details. Wish you were there with us to make it perfect. Hope your classes are going ok. Good luck to David.

Fondest love as ever,

Mumsie

14 June 1989

My Dear Laura,

I have enclosed the trousers as promised. Hope they are not too big. I also enclose the black night-shirt in case you go into hospital or something. Hope you like it. I think it is really nice. It was very expensive and then reduced to £7.99 – the trousers were reduced to £14.99 but *please* don't hold onto them if you don't like them. I can't afford to hold onto things you won't wear any more.

Enclosed are 13 x 14p stamps which I bought for you. If you don't like either thing, return it to me by 29th June – the £1.54 should be enough. Ask them how much at

---

[24] Mum won a competition in the *Edinburgh Evening News* for dinner for two at the Caledonian Hotel.

the Post Office. Say you have some stamps to use up and stick them on. You may manage to save a few stamps. If you decide to keep the goods, keep the stamps for letter writing.

I have put them in a little container so that you won't lose them. I am not sure what kind of a rash you have on your legs but if it's a sweat rash, enclosed baby cream should help. Also some antiseptic Savlon, which may help. I am sure your deodorant will be finished and talc, so I have also enclosed some I had for you in your goody bag. You can buy replacements when you get cash – ha ha. It will help you keep cool and fresh.

I also enclose cheese, savoury sauce, sweeteners and a packet of luxury chicken and sweetcorn soup – you liked it at Easter. I hope these might save you a little cash. I had a little money saved to buy you new winter shoes at the sales and maybe a couple of tops and some knickers but I hope the sales won't be over when you come home.

You will really have to get your act in order a bit more next term Laura and try to do a bit more action and less pipe-dreaming. You must find out for yourself what is due to you – rail fares, dentist (and please go there), sign on for any social benefits or housing benefits. And work in the summer must be your priority – *not* a week with this one, a week with that one – waiting for someone to collect your luggage, leaving studies until just before exams. I will be out of action for 3 months when op time comes. I am not sure if I will ever work again afterwards. It is doubtful but I would like to know you were self-sufficient. You should be able to send your own thank-you notes and remember when people's birthdays are without me sending you the cards. You must try very hard, Laura. I am very, very tired and work takes a really supreme effort nowadays. I have almost been on my knees this past 2 weeks doing double shifts in this heat. The doctors say I must take tomorrow off and rest in bed all day. Dad does all the work – cooking, doing the shopping, cleaning the house, making the beds and hanging out the washing, the dishes, all before going to work at 10.30 a.m. I only do a little ironing. No egg shells in the eggs any more. He painted the bathroom and sitting room the second week of his holidays.

I had quite a nice birthday. I was not looking forward to it. Mum and Dad and Laura missing. Morag's girls don't give us presents any more. Dear Dad gave me my favourite lipstick and Crabtree and Evelyn talc. It was sweet. He only has £5 a week pocket money now and must have been saving hard as the lipstick is £7 and talc £4. I remembered all the little goodies Mum used to have for me, and a birthday cake, when I visited them on my birthday. (No-one ever loves you like your mum.) Margaret gave me a wooden egg cup (a present from Seafield) and a milk jug (minus the sugar basin) and the perfume I had given her as a little extra for Christmas.

One other sad thing. I arrived at work to find someone was sick and I had to go back and work until 7 p.m.

The nice things. The little girl who sometimes helps me at work and is really hard up. She works with us through the day (part-time) and with a chip shop at night and weekends to save for a deposit on a little house. She discovered it was my birthday and came back with a beautiful card and magnetic teddy for the freezer. It was so sweet of her. I was really crying.

When I got home at lunchtime I found your special delivery fruit and lovely card awaiting me (and I thought you had forgotten Mumsie). I sat and cried. I knew you wouldn't forget.

I arranged the box of fruit in a really posh basket with bows and ribbons and said to everyone, 'Look what Laura sent – she does love me after all.' How thoughtful of you to know I loved kiwi fruit. Only Dad knew that. Did he tell you?[25] They were delicious and the melon, apples, peaches and mandarins and surprise, surprise the very first card I ever received from you that said, 'To the best mum in the world' with roses and bluebirds and hearts. I went back to work in the afternoon, walking on air. My little girl had not forgotten her old mum. The day was lovely after that. Ian brought me 2 lovely Dutch prints which I adored, and cash. We quickly drank wine, played music. Dad was so sweet (as always). I felt loved again and as a bonus, next day another present from my baby. Her usual funny card, funny pressie and lovely letter, which I read 100 times and read to everyone. I was so happy you were having a lovely time. David sounds so

---

[25] Dad had assumed I would forget mum's birthday and bought the basket and fruit and written a card in disguised writing so she would not feel disappointed. I'd not forgotten though, so she got two presents from me in the end.

nice and I feel I know his mum already. She sounds a really sweet lady. I am dying to meet David.

I am sorry I sound such a misery tonight. I should have waited until tomorrow, when I was having the day off and didn't feel like a wrung-out chamois.

I just worry such a lot about the future – ours and yours. I want you to have a good life, a happy life. I wish I could shelter you from all the storms but realise that this is not possible and I feel frustrated that I cannot build a 10-foot wall to keep you and Dad safe from the hurts of life. The Never Never Land, Camelot, Shangri-La would be my choice for you. But I realise I do not have the strength to make this possible for you both. I also realise that I have been oh so very lucky to have had a wonderful doting grandma, the most wonderful parents ever second to none and in spite of wealthy, intelligent, witty, ambitious suitors, I married the poor one. But I realise so very late in life he was the richest in love, compassion, understanding, determination and tolerance. (And must have been a saint to put up with me and my pipe dreams all those years. It couldn't have been easy.) And he gave me the greatest prize of my whole life – my Laura, my joy, my pride, my frustration, my vexation, my enigma, my soul mate in music, literature and art, my love, my torment, my darling, my life and eventually my whole purpose for living.

Everything in my life had seemed meaningless before 2 December 1966 and everything afterwards seemed to centre around you. You are so important to me (what a burden to give a child). I do not ever want to possess you (that is not love – that is selfishness). I let you go last year gracefully because that is what love is about but I do want you to make the most of your wonderful gifts (not material – intellectual). I know we learn by our mistakes but try not to make too many. Everything comes to she who waits but you have already waited quite a while and you have to give fate a hand occasionally. Basically, Laura, I would not like you to have to work so long or so hard as I have or have to struggle. You have it academically but as yet, you do not have the aggression to go out and get it. You can do it (this past year has proven that fact to me). The world is your oyster. You are young, healthy and clever. Grasp it, for that is your security for the future and I am sure you have realised in the past year that it is impossible to be a 100% idealist in a materialistic world. You must resign yourself to a halfway measure. I think that is where I went wrong. I should have played the 'middle of the field' and life would have been more tranquil – not challenging – but tranquil, and there is a peace of mind in finding a secure job with a pension, 2.5 babies, a semi-detached in suburbia, a car, 2 holidays abroad per annum – you don't get ulcers and regrets in your 50s.

Oh hell, I should have written this tomorrow. Anyway you wouldn't be a fruit-and-nut-case like,

Your loving Mumsie

Who still (and always will) loves and misses you. Sorry.

1989, PART TWO

The Twilight Zone

Just before I returned home for the summer in 1989, mum finally got the date through for her heart surgery – 24 August. Although daunted by the anticipation of such a major operation, mum, as usual, was happy with this date as it meant that the weather would still be warm for dad going up to visit her, I'd still be home so could help out, she could continue to work at the surgery over the summer and make the most of the seasonal lodgers to save a bit of money to help keep things ticking over when she was recuperating.

While I was home I managed to get some regular temping work with an agency in town, which gave her slightly less to worry about and meant I wasn't moping around the house all day.

I visited David at his parents' home near Melton Mowbray and he came up to Edinburgh a couple of times. Mum being mum insisted on taking him on her tour of the Royal Mile and generally fussing over us when she should have been resting and preparing herself for the operation. Mum really hit it off with David and enjoyed talking about poetry with him and nursing him with her home-made medications when he got an eye infection. Mum had drawers full of free samples of drugs she'd been given by medical reps at work and was forever dispensing remedies for everything from diarrhoea to arthritic pain to friends and relatives. I remember when I was younger my friend Anne got a terrible attack of ear-ache when she was round at our house one night. Mum gave her two DF118s and she was instantly cured and incredibly stoned.

David and I had decided to get a flat together in London when we returned, as rooms in the halls of residence were only available to students during their first year. Also, as David had now finished his final exams and was looking for work in London, it seemed like an ideal point to finally find a flat of our own. Mum was in favour of us finding somewhere to stay together but in retrospect, the last thing she needed as the operation got closer was the extra stress of me once again trying to find somewhere to live, four hundred miles away.

Mum underwent heart surgery on 24 August 1989 – a mitral valve replacement. Having suffered a childhood bout of rheumatic fever, she frequently suffered from heart problems and related illnesses, undoubtedly brought on by stress (of which I was a major contributing factor), overwork and a shocking addiction (which I share) to cigarettes. Dad stopped smoking in the early 1970s after mum decided they couldn't afford for both of them to have the habit.

The operation took place in the old Edinburgh Royal Infirmary, a place we'd all become very familiar with over the years through various members of the family spending time there. Mum used to joke that she spent so much time in there they should give her her own bed. As usual, mum spent much of the days leading up to the op making friends with the other patients and staff, making everyone laugh, enjoying having new people to regale with her anecdotes and stories, as well as keeping the many people who went up to visit her entertained, gossiping about one lot of visitors with the next. If she was afraid, she never showed it, being more concerned about whether I was helping dad, we were eating and bathing regularly and most of all, if and when she could get back to her beloved job at the doctors' surgery. When she was in hospital, dad and I would share the household tasks, him doing the breakfast and me making something for tea, trying to keep up with the washing and tidying and trying to make sure one of us was up there for both of the two daily visiting hours. Aside from this, I can't remember giving dad much support. As usual, I bottled all my fears and emotions up and forgot to ask him how he was feeling.

The night before the operation, mum gave me the following letter which she'd written in the hospital.

From Mumsie (soon to be New Mumsie),

Dear Little Girl,

Well, when you read this we will have said 'Goodbye' and the next time we say 'Hello' you will have a Bionic Mum.

Not to worry. I feel quite calm. Go and have your hair done Thursday night and surprise me on Friday in Intensive Care.

Keep the washing down and iron everything and look a credit to Mumsie.

Well I have had physios, anaesthetists, radiographers, the surgeon, a blessing from the local Catholic priest who is coming to see me off from 7 a.m. onwards tomorrow, the local rabbi from *Fiddler on the Roof*, the hospital chaplain, a support group from Cardiacs Anonymous – something like Alcoholics Anonymous, you know – 'We had a rotten heart like you but we licked it. Can we help you?' Nice though.

Margaret in the next bed is getting a pig's valve. I am having a metal one. Hers snorts – mine clicks, forever more, rather like the crocodile in *Peter Pan*. I can never play hide and seek again, ticking in a cupboard like a time-bomb, can I? I asked if I would set off the alarms at the airport going through Customs. 'Just show him your scar,' he said. Who wants to do a topless at Customs?

Well my wee girl, I hope all goes well for you and you can manage to do all the needful with Mum being out of reach for a few days. You can pop in Friday night. I may still be in I.C., wired up with tubes – no, 2nd thoughts, it may be better you don't see me like that. Saturday, I will be longing to see you and your lucky horseshoe will bring me luck.

I love you and am proud of you, Laura. Please help Dad all you can. He can't detach himself like you. We go back a long way he and I (good days and bad).

Margaret in the next bed said, 'What a beautiful girl Laura is. A face full of character. The doctor couldn't keep his eyes off her.' So there. You are my inheritance to you – beauty, brains, 5 gold rings, 4 calling birds, 3 French hens, £2000 income bonds and a kettle and a colour TV. Only joking, honest. (It rhymes anyway.)

I am not so scared, now – Que Será Será.

Try not to let Dad feel depressed on Friday and the weekend. I will be looking b***** awful – no make-up, no deodorant or talc even – stinky pooh.

Darling, must go and have a shave. Take care until Mummy returns from the Twilight Zone.

Your loving Mumsie xxx

I went up to the hospital with dad to visit mum in Intensive Care the night of the operation. She wasn't conscious but it was just such a relief to see her, the operation she'd waited years for now in the past. Dad and I sat with her for a while, nervously watching the various monitors, trying to fathom what they all did. Mum was in a room with about eight other people who had had major surgery that day. The only sounds were those of the various machines. It was a strange, not quite living, atmosphere. I knew mum was still coming round from the anaesthetic but I just wanted her to be able to speak to us, or communicate in some way. Just so we knew when they'd opened up her heart, part of that unique thing that was June Hird hadn't been removed or altered in any way. Mum looked jaundiced and vulnerable, but peaceful.

Mum's first words to me after she came round from the operation were 'Have a perm.' I knew immediately the old June was back. Me getting my hair permed was something of a family joke after mum had given me a home perm in my early teens. She thought it looked lovely but I'd walked about with the hood of my cagoule up for several weeks after. In retrospect, as she'd just gone through major surgery, it wouldn't have hurt me to go to the hairdresser and give her a surprise, but the first time had been traumatic enough.

The hospital recommended a recuperation period of at least three months after the operation, but mum being mum was back to work within five weeks. She just couldn't keep away. The time I was home during the five weeks she did not rest, could not keep still and was probably working as hard around the house as she would have been at work. Friends and relatives would bring round things they'd cooked for her, dad would make his hearty soups and I was able to experiment with meals, having finally learned to cook for myself over the past year. Mum pretended to enjoy her introduction to soya, tuna pasta, etc. and the other ghastly student fare I served up for her and dad. Before I left to go back to London, she'd also started taking the occasional lodger again, unable to resist the tail end of the Edinburgh Festival summer season, and never wanting to let down Cam when her own guest house was full; grateful for all the guests Cam had sent to us over the years.

I can't remember how quickly mum started smoking again after the operation but dog-ends in the back green and the smell of smoke in the bathroom after she'd been in started to give the game away. I couldn't criticise. I was doing the same thing, in the same clandestine places, also having pretended I'd stopped to encourage mum to continue to do the same.

When I moved back down to London after the summer, I moved into a flat in Highbury with David, which we shared with a journalist and photographer. David had graduated by this time, and the rent was high (£440 a month for a double room which didn't have a bed – only a bed settee – a real bone of contention for mum). He took various temping jobs, and eventually a part-time job in a children's bookshop in Islington (£130 a week) for a couple of months. In October 1989 I started working as a relief cashier for Ladbrokes Racing for twenty-one hours each week. I was based all over North London – Hampstead Heath, Archway, Kentish Town, Holloway Road, etc. and loved all the characters, the gambling addicts, the earthy bookies' staff. Even though it usually involved at least an hour of travelling at the beginning and end of each day I didn't mind as I enjoyed this too — it offered me a further chance to people-watch and enjoy the sights and sounds of a London that was still new and exciting to me. I would also bunk off lectures if I was offered extra hours.

Mum was pleased that I'd finally done something positively independent as she frequently (as the letters show) encouraged/nagged me to find work over the course of my life. Then she started worrying that I wasn't spending enough time on my studies.

Within a few short weeks of mum returning to work after the operation, she began to notice a deterioration in her short-term memory. Aside from having to cope with the computerisation of the surgery in her absence, the massive changes that the NHS was undergoing at the time, and having to do regular double shifts, it became clear that part of her memory had been damaged during the operation. Mum tried to talk to me about these new fears during phone calls and in the letters, not wanting to worry dad, but I was so caught up in a new chapter in my life I once again failed to give her the support she craved. Part of me believed her insistence on returning to work way in advance of the recommended recuperation period was more to blame than the operation itself. I buried my head back in the sand when mum needed me most and let her down again.

Tuesday, 11 October 1989

My Dearest Laura,

My first letter to your new abode. Hope you and David are enjoying 'playing houses'. I am sure you are excelling at the cooking – I certainly enjoyed everything you made when you were home. When did you learn your culinary accomplishments? Please bear with me if my writing, spelling and punctuation are a bit under the weather. I am sure I left part of my brain in surgery – my God, this is all one paragraph. Am I turning into Virginia Wolff? (2 Fs or 1 – not sure.)

I hope David is lucky with his interviews. I am sure he will be and would be an asset to any firm. He certainly would have impressed me on the times when I did personnel. I know I would be saying immediately, 'He is the one for the job.' Good luck to him and to you when you look for temp work. The agencies are bursting at the seams with temp work in Edinburgh, so I can imagine what London must be like.

You will be back to college today. I was thinking of you and hoping you liked Enfield. I hope you will study hard this year (all year). You can't afford re-sits but I am sure you won't need them. As soon as you can calculate how much your fares are going to be, please let me know. I will try an appeal to South Gyle. They don't promise anything but they do not come and offer it to you if you do not ask – as we already know from last year and the travel permit.

I have missed you such a lot – missed all your caring little surprises, nursing, lovely meals and most of all laughter. There has not been much to laugh at since you left, apart from Margaret and Jack who have been splendid at taking me for runs in the car. No-one else has really cared. Probably they thought Dad was attending to me as he had 2 weeks' holiday but I have been left pretty much to my own resources (which were physically nil and emotionally very fragile) but sheer bloody-mindedness is keeping me going and I have not resorted back to smoking as a crutch.[26] It would be rather futile after 5 weeks.

I am longing to be fit, independent and back to work and then I must make some new plans for the structure of my life – a bit late in the day, perhaps, but I feel that I must make drastic changes – just what – I am still too weak to plan!!

Carole's baby will be baptised on Sunday – Lauren Emma. We have been invited to the service at St Michael's at 11 a.m. and afterwards to a knees-up and sandwich at the Orwell Lodge (one glass of wine). I would not make both but will maybe plump for the kirk service and forget the knees-up. In that way I won't be involved in the post-mortem which always follows the next day.

Subject: Who got p***** on one glass of wine? Who chatted up the waiter?

---

[26] Mum didn't realise that I knew she was secretly smoking again and I hadn't the heart to confront her in her fragile condition.

I am only choking – it will probably be fun. We haven't had a christening since Nikki. I was fairy godmother. Will let you know all about it next time.

Old Jim is coming up to Edinburgh in 2 weeks' time. I had a few minutes' absolute panic when Heather phoned me. Even with Parkinson's and 2 knee replacements and a walking stick, he can probably run faster than I can at present. I also thought he was coming to claim his case which the moths ate (remains of which were collected by the Cleansing Department the Tuesday I was admitted to hospital). Panic, panic, cold sweat, new valve bashing like blazes, felt faint, relapse – then she explained he was only staying in Edinburgh one night, with her, flying. They are staying in a hotel in Edinburgh and moving on to Inverness next day. I am to be collected by taxi at 2 p.m. to an unknown rendezvous. She refused to say where it was. I did not like to ask if I would be blindfolded. At the moment I feel so jaded, sipping pina coladas in a grass skirt in the Bahamas with old Jim would break the monotony for about 5 minutes until Sean Connery came along. Now there's another story. If I hadn't been so stuck up all these years ago when his mum invited me along to meet the young Sean Connery (alias Big Tam) because we both liked acting. I said, 'No, I am a real actress – Desdemona, Ophelia and all that.' He was just in the chorus of *South Pacific*. Ah well. Story of my life. Your mother could have been 'Pussy Galore' or more!! Choking again.

I haven't written anything for such a long time – enjoying

this – came to sitting room to escape your father. Felt like strangling him. Felt like knifing him last night. The video has conked out completely with him watering the flowers over it. He burst the 3rd swing bin in a year, took the paint off the door trying to remove the plaster with which he stuck the envelope.[27] Then he repainted the patch of plaster – THE WRONG COLOUR!!! It could cost £60 to have that door painted.

'Walk away from stress,' they say. 'All your worries and frustrations are melting away like snow on a stream, you are drifting on a white fluffy cloud, not a care in the—' That was when he switched on the spin dryer and hoover at the same time. When I consider that it was a drip-dry shirt and I had been pleading with him to hoover for 3 days, I could not believe that it was an accident.

Last night I had a double Scotch to relax – hate the taste. Had to hold my nose when I drank it, uggh, and wash away the taste with lemonade but it made me relaxed and sleepy.

But I couldn't take the nasty stuff through the day. Never mind, in 2 days' time I am returning to Ghastly Astley for relaxation classes and physio. They are taking me there and back by taxi and a lot of my friends from hospital have phoned me to check I will be there so it should be

---

[27] When I was growing up, if either mum, dad or myself had to leave the house unexpectedly we would leave a note stuck to the front door, usually with Sellotape but I take it in this instance dad hadn't been able to find Sellotape so had used sticking plaster.

fun. Really looking forward to it very much – wow-eeh, June flies over the cuckoo's nest.

Your holiday pay should be in the bank – made it up to £35 in case it was £5 digits. (Last of the big spenders.)

June S. from work called yesterday. Haven't seen Ian for ages. Will catch up with him at the baptism.

Well, when you are convalescing there is not much to write about – nothing happens.

Put your wee bits of baccy together and enclose it, or have you stopped?

I still have your lucky horseshoe. Will return it to you soon, whenever I get out of the doldrums.

T'care, keep smiling, pip pip, work hard, wash your bras and nighties, get a perm, give up the demon drink, eat well, get lots of sleep <u>AT NIGHT</u>. Give David a big hug for me and wish him all the best.

Fondest loving kisses,

From your Mumsie

P.S. Did Teddy make it back from his holiday home?

Sunday, 26 November 1989

My Dear Wee Girl,

Here are the tights as promised. Hope they are big enough. I enclose a finer pair also, plus your baccy in advance, plus a little something to give your lentil soup a boost.

I worry about you sounding so tired and not being able to get your books read because you are working so hard. Your college work must come before everything but I know you know that. I admire you for your fierce determination to be independent but do not make yourself ill doing more than you should. Look where it landed me.

Enough of the lecture. We had a super, giggly, boozy, well-fed night at Ian's. Alan has fractured his heel so he was plastered before we started. Alan's Mum and Dad were there and everyone was asking for you. Alan always says you are the brightest, wittiest girl he knows. Maybe he doesn't know many but I always like to hear people praise my lassie.

I have a new word to add to your list of Mumsie quotes. When anyone asks with whom Laura is staying, I always say, 'David,' and the nosy ones who say, 'David, is he her fiancé? Her lover?' I say, her 'bidey-in'. It was an expression from Aberdeen that Dr W used to use a lot and when I asked what he meant, he said, 'When 2 people who are not married live together, you say that to nosy-parkers, "He's my bidey-in."'

In case you find life a wee bit dull when you are home, we have arranged a party (pre-Christmas) for Ian, Alan, Alan's Mum and Dad and a few other people to meet you and David.

Poem enclosed.

For Laura

I remember a moment one December
My brain was in a whirl
My empty arms now promised wonder
I had a baby girl

I remember all the lonely years
I thought my life was fine
No precious gift in all the world
Compared with baby mine

I remember stories that we shared
And Poems oft times told
The music in my darling's soul
Brought Pappa years of gold

I remember taking my girl to school
A golden scholar she
Took pride in all creative things
And created pride in me

I remember long, frustrating years
My darling child was sad
Somehow she could not talk to me
Sorry if I seemed mad

I remember now that golden day
She woke from hibernation
And planned a future for her life
Rejecting her frustration

I remember well when she left home
For life in London town
My baby now was growing up
I must not feel so down

I remember a station parting
Some tears, a sniff, a blink
Her treasures in two suitcases
Plus her teddy and kitchen sink!!!

I remember that my golden girl
Will soon be twenty-three
It seems like only yesterday
She sat upon my knee

Remember that you hold my heart
My child with golden aura
I am proud to know that I'm the mum
Of a girl whom we called Laura

I worry about you feeling ill and not looking after yourself. I am longing for you to be home to take care of you – even for a little while. Please take care my little one. You are all I have and are very precious.

The cough bottle will help. Take hot drinks with 2 Co-proxamol or the Panadol.

Have a good birthday. I will be thinking of you all day. Thinking of the first time, 23 years ago, I said, 'Hi, little girl, you are the best thing that ever happened to me.'

Hope David enjoys his new job and you have lots of happiness in your new flat. And that you can concentrate when you return to London to settling down to your studies with no worries. I know the past few months have been touchy. You deserve a break now.

There are no pressies enclosed as you are moving house. I have some goodies at home for you.

Fondest love, as always,

Mumsie

Tuesday, 12 December 1989

Dear Laura,

It is 5 a.m. Can't sleep. Too tired, I think. Those double shifts coming now seem to be the straw that broke the camel's back.

I suddenly realised after you rang off last night that your Christmas visit home had been shortened yet again. It hardly seems worth it, does it?

My whole life recently has been revolving around your visit home, ticking the days off on the calendar, filling the freezer full of goodies. I offered to make up your lost wages if you could make it a little longer.

It seems such a long time since I saw you. Even Jonathan stays longer.[28]

However, I am not going to get involved in cheap emotional blackmail.

Presents are not important. Seeing you is but there is no point in coming home out of a sense of duty and keep chopping off more and more days.

Please don't try to sweeten me by having me look

---

[28] Margaret and Jack's son. See Characters list at end.

forward to a mid-term week. You know you would probably change your mind at the last moment.

This is probably not a very good time to write to you. I am feeling tired, down and feel particularly rejected by the family and will probably regret writing a hurtful letter to you immediately after posting it.

I just feel you could have spared us a week, had a good rest and given us some time to chat and maybe have some friends over for a little party to say 'Hello'. There just won't be time.

Sorry.

Mum

P.S. I didn't take it in. Are you arriving Christmas Eve and leaving 28th now??

1990, PART ONE

Come Back Little Sheba

Just before going home for Christmas, Ladbrokes told me
I would have to work New Year's Day so I had to go back
down to London before Hogmanay. Mum was really upset
that I'd miss being with them her first New Year after
surgery, but I'd agreed in my contract to work public holidays, and as I was now used to the extra money from the
bookies, did not want to jeopardise it. Plus, I felt I was only
doing what she'd always told me to do.

We still managed to have some good times while I
was home, having friends and family round, watching
videos together, going out for runs with Margaret and
Jack, Margaret taking me out for coffee and cake and
a chat. (I was very close to mum's friend Margaret and
she was one of the few people at the time and up until
her death in 2002 in whom I felt I could truly trust
and confide.) During a party at the house on Boxing
Day, one of the guests had picked on dad, and myself
and my friend Anne's boyfriend at the time had stuck
up for him. I couldn't remember ever having stuck up
for my dad before. In the few days after, prior to me

going back to London, a new kind of closeness seemed to develop between us. It was like he'd finally found the daughter that he'd needed around him earlier in the year during mum's operation. When mum came to see me off at the station on 29 December, dad turned up to say *bon voyage* having managed to get a couple of hours off work. We parted on good terms and I phoned them both from the phone box in East Finchley High Street for the bells on Hogmanay.

Towards the end of 1989, David and I had moved from the flat in Highbury to a shared flat in East End Road in East Finchley. Whilst staying at the Highbury flat I had started suffering from panic attacks partly due to the fact the flat was in the middle of a red-light district and I was constantly harassed by kerb crawlers. The rent on the new flat was half of the £440 a week for a room we had previously been paying. David continued working in the children's bookshop, despite hating it, and I continued to study and work at Ladbrokes. Neither of us having lived with a partner before, or shared a room, we argued frequently. There were also troubles with me still seeing all our old friends when I was at polytechnic, and him feeling isolated, working in a different part of London.

At the end of January, David suffered a breakdown. On the night everything came to a head, as our room had sustained some damage and some of the other flat-mates had become involved and upset, our landlord asked us to leave. David went back to his parents' house in Melton Mowbray to recuperate and I was left to find somewhere else to live, not knowing whether he was going to return or not.

Having spent several weeks trawling round North London trying to find a new flat, I went home for a few days around 5 February. Mum, dad and Margaret helped me phone round places and generally gave me their welcome shoulders to cry on. Despite mum's own health and work concerns she devoted all her free time to trying to help sort things out for me and even arranged for me to see a counsellor at the poly when I got back down. I managed to convince my landlord from East Finchley to let me stay on at the flat until I found somewhere else and in the end I stayed on until the summer holidays.

David and I remained, and still remain, friends. He eventually ended up at York University where he studied for his Masters, and subsequent PhD in Philosophy. He now lives back in London where he writes and occasionally lectures.

7 January 1990

My Dearest Wee Girl,
Well, it is Sunday and the 7th day into a new year and new decade and I still have not written to you to give you details of our glowing social life since you departed for London, nor have I imparted any pearls of wisdom from the school of experience of my working-class background

(born with a wooden spoon and not a silver one orally in situ).

So here is Mumsie once more in her favourite (if not frequent) pastime of writing to you, fortified by 2 plates of Dad's chicken broth and a thickly filled chicken roll, garnished with cranberry sauce. Thought of getting in touch with old Pan Am Bob to try and arrange a twice-weekly delivery of Dad's soup to you but their planes sometimes have difficulty in making it over the border and it would be an awful waste of good soup, so will have to make soup every day when you are home.[29] Just asked Dad what he thought about this and he said 'Souper' or was it 'Super'? Sounds the same.

Errol Flynn is on in the background sorting out the Wild West with Randolph Scott. (Did you know Randy was gay??)

We miss you lots as always and Anne said to me an Edinburgh without Laura is a dull place, but you would probably find Auld Reekie a dull place now if you were here permanently. I was so pleased and surprised to see Dad waiting at the station when we arrived last Friday. He didn't even hint that he might try – nice guy, isn't he? –

---

[29] During the time I was involved with Bob prior to going down to London, on the night of one of his planned visits up to Edinburgh, the Lockerbie disaster had taken place. As he worked for Pan Am, his visit was cancelled. Scottish humour being black as it is, mum and I used to joke that Bob had somehow arranged Lockerbie so he could get out of coming to see me.

still chuffed about your moral support on Boxing Day. Margaret and Jack came over on New Year's Day for drinkies and a buffet and lots of Nat King Cole-ing – 'Mona Lisa', 'When I Fall in Love' etc., etc. It was pleasant and you were talked about frequently in glowing terms. I think Margaret has adopted you since your chat. She and Jack and Sylvia have great hopes for you academically. I enclose this little note they posted to me just after Christmas. Jack's message on one side, Margaret's on the other, so you will know I did not make it up. I think Margaret's is really sweet. The Libby she refers to is her eldest grand-daughter, who lives near London.

Haven't seen the family (no first-footing like in Grandma and Pappa's day) but they phone every day. Ian and Hopalong[30] took Alan's parents to a posh 3-day hotel New Year celebration – 4-course breakfast, 3-course lunch, 5-course dinner, champagne galore. Cost Ian a small fortune . . .

Dad and I have just been enjoying a quiet life, watching videos (got it fixed) and listening to Nat King Cole, eating when we are hungry, working, wearing my new white sweater and gloves (often). Finished our Bailey's – mmmh. Stopped drinking wine but have 1 small nip of whisky with lots of ice and Diet Sprite for a good night's sleep.

Nikki has apparently been struggling with the sociology, even though she studies every night until 11 p.m. and 12 hours Saturday and Sunday in a beautiful new study they

---

[30] Alan, whose leg was still in plaster.

had made for her and her mother does all her washing and cooking and she never needs to take a bus. She borrows her mother's car or her father drives her everywhere. Poor little bugger. I wonder how she would cope with a job in Ladbrokes, travelling and living in London, doing her own shopping, cooking, washing and budgeting. It is a pity she did not take up your offer to see her at Christmas. She also would have realised how the other half live. However, my darling, when you come to write your best-seller, you will be rich with experience of life, although you have paid dearly for it.

Dad and I visited a few sales yesterday. Dad spent his birthday money on 2 pairs of shoes.[31] I bought 2 new pans (non-stick so far), guaranteed to last a lifetime (felt I deserved a further discount at my age). We also bought the enclosed cardi – hope you like it. Couldn't get black but this one is dark, roomy, warm and should go with your skirts and trousers. Sorry I ruined your other one. I will try to get you another blouse before sales finish.

I am going to visit the psychologist at Neurology again on Wednesday to try to locate my lost memory. She is really helpful. You really must try and make time to visit your counsellor as soon as possible. It does help. She told me that I tried too hard to please everyone and make everyone happy and help everyone to my own detriment.

---

[31] Had given dad some money for his birthday on 28 May while I was home as I had a little extra from working at Ladbrokes and knew I'd be broke by the time his birthday actually arrived.

'Look out for yourself,' she said. 'Do the best for yourself, in that way you will be strong mentally and physically. You can't please everyone. You are important to you. The people you are trying to please won't give a jot if you are down.' She did not mean Dad and you. We are all in the same canoe. She meant going back to work too early, trying to please my friends and family and not being able to say, 'No, I am living my own life.' I wish I had had advice like this a long time ago. I would have studied more, stayed on at school, not hung around too long in dead-end jobs, taken more chances re buying a bigger house with a view to starting a real guest house (no worry about bosses or redundancy). Would have gone abroad sooner and seen the world but I did not have much confidence in myself. Drama school was another dream.

I realise that it is a bit late in the day to change but I can still improve the quality of what is left.

Tomorrow you go back to college, baby. See the counsellor. You have been working much too hard, little one. Harder than you should ever need. I had not realised how much you had grown up, how tired you looked, how much I admired you and loved you. (No, that is not true. I always knew how much I loved you from day one and before.) However, you simply <u>must</u> apply yourself to your studies and give priority to this. You have an excellent brain and I know if the circumstances were different and you did not have all those other niggling worries devouring your energy and your feeling of security you could eat those exams and essays. You are working too hard on other things. Do you really need to work 3 days at Ladbrokes? Would Friday and Saturday not suffice? Or just Saturday?? I know I am sounding like the nagging Mum. I don't want to be this. Graduation to you is important. You sacrificed and put up with more than anyone should to make it this far. The chance will not come again and I would not like you to spend your life thinking of what 'might have been' because circumstances made you over-tired, over-anxious because of financial worries. Dad and I can come to some arrangement to help you financially if you wish.

If you would like me to add something to David's CV I will do it for you to save you time. It would look better on the electric typewriter. I am not as good a typist as you are but I am not too bad. Don't worry, we will give him a good character reference when called upon. It might be quite a good idea if David is interested in a Civil Service career to apply to the top Civil Service department directly. Home Office or Foreign Office. I know all the departments are listed under Scottish Office, St Andrews House for Edinburgh in telephone directory. It may be Whitehall in London. I know they accept new applicants several times a year. Do you remember you were due to sit the Home Office exam on the week you started at Kinnear & Gordon? David may not need to sit an exam being a graduate but I am not sure.

It is a very secure job, good salary, good holidays, good chance of promotion, chance to be an MP and write novels e.g. Jeffrey Archer or autobiography – Winston Churchill, Harold MacMillan, Harold Wilson, Jennie Lee,

Anthony Eden – definitely worth a try. Good luck, Sir David. Definitely could foresee a great future.

Well my darling. Back to earth for you and me. *Antiques Roadshow* just finished now. I must take Robert Burns and Peter Pan plus Currer Bell and Bernadette to meet them in Edinburgh – plus 5 gold rings.[32]

Whilst we are on the subject, *Reader's Digest* Draw in final stages (isn't it always?). I have it in your name, darling. (Will you share the £150,000 with us? Halfers?) You can have the car (I will give you the key). You and I can have the Caribbean holiday together (we need it). I told them you would like to accept the cheque from a celebrity (preferably Dennis Nilsen in London). Is that ok? Remember halfers. £75,000 each. Enough for a 'but and ben' in Wimbledon for you and a guest house in Edinburgh for us. You will get it all back eventually. I just want to know what to do in case Sir Harry Secombe phones.

Good luck my lovely – one good thing you have <u>your</u> confidence in <u>you</u>. I am proud of that.

Dad has brought some tinned mackerel on toast.

Love and big kisses,

Mumsie xxxx

Dad xxx [*In dad's handwriting*]

---

[32] Mum loved collecting rare books from jumble sales and charity shops. She didn't do so with any real view to selling them, but more as a collector/hoarder, however she used to say that she would take them along to *Antiques Roadshow* if it visited Edinburgh to hopefully prove what a shrewd eye she had for a bargain.

[*Post-it note attached*]

Dear Laura,
Enclosed rugby shirts. If you like them both just keep them.
If you don't like either put in correct bags – returned goods
receipt on respective bags, and enclose in Peter Craig
envelope. Free address label on front. Take to Post Office
– <u>soon</u>. Nothing to pay. Ink-in catalogue numbers on
address label. If you only like <u>one</u> put one you don't like
in the right bag and do same as above. Rub out catalogue
number you are keeping. Ink in other. Hope you like them
– remember to Sellotape bag before returning it. Have a
nice time with Anne. Bought Scottish Cheddar for you today.
    Luv Mumsie xxx

25 January 1990

My Darling Wee Girlie,
It is a blooming cold Friday afternoon as you probably
know, so I am back from work and am going to get this
letter (which I intended writing last night) off to you before
the 5 o'clock shift. The contents are too precious to go
astray.
    After you telephoned last night and I sensed oh-so-well
that you were ill, tired, hungry, lonely, sad, frustrated,
afraid, all the feelings I wish I could magic away for you,
my first reaction was to take a few days' leave (which I
can still do, if you just say the word), come down to
London, wrap you up, pack your things and bring you

home, where I can look after you and give you a good rest until you feel strong enough to think straight again.

During this time, Margaret phoned to find out if there was any news from you. Incidentally, she is the *only* one who knows David has gone home. She loves you so much, it wouldn't have been fair not to share your trials as well as your tribulations. She is like a second Mum to you. I have not mentioned anything to anyone else.

Margaret is worried and anxious for you and angry with the fact that you are alone in London with far too many responsibilities and a hell of a lot of guts and natural talent which fate seems to be intent on bashing and never really seems to be giving you a chance to get on your feet. She agreed with me that you need some help and advice, either via the college, certainly a doctor about your health, even Citizens' Advice. I know all those things take time and time is not on your side at present but here are some other suggestions.

1 Suggestions if staying on in London

    a. Hostel accommodation. YWCA or some other hostel such as that other one. At least you would be warm, fed and would have peace to study and company would be there if you needed it. If this appeals to you and it would only need to be until exams, ask the college to organise it for you. You don't have the time to wander around in the cold, or the money for the fares and telephone. I can ask David's mum to collect his things from the flat.

b. You would definitely be entitled to a rent allowance if you decided on a nice flat. If you were granted this, please drop Ladbrokes or at least only work on Friday or Saturday to give yourself a chance to catch up. Ask the college for help with rent allowance. It may take a little while to organise. We could help you out until then.

c. Keep pestering college accommodation people next week. Don't waste your own time and energy trailing on fruitless tasks.

2. Suggestions if you decide to return to Scotland

a. Ask college if you can transfer your course to home base to complete. Surely with all the difficulties you have had to encounter they would make enquiries at least for you. It may not be possible to do this for this year but application could be made now for September.

b. Ask if you could come home and study and get your essays up to date and return to London for the exams. When you pass this year you can get yourself better organised for the final year. It would cost nothing to stay at home. You would probably still be entitled to some sort of grant. (Even if you came home to study until after Easter!!!)

c. Just call it a day and come home for good. Have a good rest then take a job and maybe do a word processing or computer course at night school to get a better job. You could write freelance. There is the typewriter here. I am sure this is the option which would least appeal to you, except if you felt you had just had enough but I wanted to include it to let you know the door of home is always open and we have worked out worse problems together. Your happiness and future are the most important things to Dad and me. We have had our life. We want yours to be rosier.

The college must take some responsibility. You spent the first year on a safe campus in pleasant surroundings with college security guards, no need to leave the campus, and when you did you had the safety of a group. Second year you're uprooted to grotty surroundings, had to join the rat race of money-grabbing landlords, forced to travel alone for the first time in London (hence the panic attacks), forced to work to keep a roof over your head. David was not the college's fault but he was another worry for you. If you wanted me to find out from this end re your entitlement to finish your degree course, I shall start fighting now. Starting with that teacher mucking up your UA application.[33]

Good grief, time is marching on, darling. While Margaret was on the phone, Anne and Douglas came in. I was so

---

[33] The teacher from my old high school whom I'd asked to write my reference was a lovely man, but accidentally mislaid my UCCA form. The real reason I didn't get into any of the universities I applied for was more to do with me not having the appropriate qualifications. In retrospect I wouldn't have wanted to study anywhere other than Middlesex Polytechnic anyway.

glad to see them. Margaret phoned back to speak to Anne. She (Margaret) feels you were left holding the baby after David left but I don't want to look back on 'ifs and buts'. The present and the future are the important things and how we channel them. Remember, darling, you are *not alone* although you must feel it just now. We are all concerned about your welfare. Anne and Douglas sat for a couple of hours. We had a bottle of wine and Douglas some beers. Needless to say, the conversation was 95% Laura.

We all like David very much and think you were good for one another but you had too much on your plate already to cope with his problems when they got out of control.

Darling, this is a lot of drivel but hope it might help in some way. Remember I *can* come down to London at any time you need me and your room is here.

Also, please phone every day just now and I will ring back. To hell with the bill. Even if you want to ring a couple of times at night. Mumsie's here to kiss it better and advise in any way I can.

I enclose Jim's £5 and will send a thank-you note for you to send him in a couple of days.

Also enclosed, claim for travelling. I have put your student ref. no. on form in case you have forgotten it. Charge for 4 days travelling per week, even if you were travelling to Ladbrokes. Try and get it off right away while you are still at your present address.

Wish I could hug you and hold you just now. I love you, darling. The sun will shine again. All my love and kisses.

Mumsie XXXX

Sunday, 28 February 1990

My Darling Wee Girl
Courage ma petite. You are constantly in my thoughts, awake or sleeping. I hope this week is 100% happier for you. It certainly could not be as bad as last week. Brighter days are ahead, I know.

First get your health sorted out and I pray you can be kept on at Finchley and get college sorted out. Just had an Inspiration. I have a full course of Amoxycillin 500mg caps which I have to keep in the fridge. (I can always get more if I get an infection.) Take 3 a day before food. Those are strong and should clear the infection quicker than 250mg which doc would probably give you but 250mg would not be strong enough for your chest. The only snag is it is a penicillin which used to give you thrush. I enclosed the Daktarin cream the doctor gave you before in case. I think I must have given you the last pessary when you were home some time. Those are in case you can't make it to the doctor's. Remember to tell him that penicillin used to give you thrush.

Oh wee girlie, I wish I could magic all your problems away but it won't be long until Easter and brighter days and remember I am always here to come to you, to come home to, or just to have a good old cry on the phone to.

Old Jim phoned me this morning to ask if I got the money and he asked if Heather had sent your birthday money, as you always write and let him know when you get money. So I explained and have enclosed a letter on your behalf explaining, also thanking him for the last £5 sent last week and sent to you. It is stamped. You just need to post it and that's another worry off your back.

Keep your chin up, my pet. Hope you soon feel better. Please don't work too hard at Ladbrokes.

Daddy sends his love to his wee girl.

My love as always and ever,

Mumsie xxx

[*Letter I wrote to mum and dad in March 1990. The only one I wrote from London that I've been able to find.*]

Friday, 8 March 1990

Hallo wee mummy and wee daddy,

It's twenty past twelve and I'm listening to the soundtrack of *Sweet Charity* and having a wee beer. I've just spent the last 4 hours retyping and sending off my women's magazine short story that I had to do for Practice of Writing, to *Bella*, *Best* and *Woman's Story Magazine* in the hope that one of them will publish me and give me a wee bit money. I changed the bits that the editor of *Woman's Realm* didn't like so hopefully I'll have a bit more luck this time. I've sent SAEs to get them sent to Edinburgh should they not publish them so you can let me know. By the way, my *nom de plume* is June Hamilton. I sat for ages trying to think of what I should call myself. I was going to make it Annie Hamilton in memory of grandma, but Annie is not a popular name to sell magazines these days, and

I thought that if my wee mummy didn't have the confidence to write her things (better than mine as they are do it again mum, you still haven't told the world about the Royal Mile when you were young) then I'd have to do it for her. If they are published you can say they are yours if you like because, in a way, they are.

I can't stop writing at the moment. I was going to go to the local cinema tonight, got halfway along the road and thought, I'd rather stay in and write something. I'm very inspired. I miss everyone but at the moment I'm glad I didn't (or you didn't persuade me to) come back home and give everything up that night the electricity was buggered. All three of us have been through horrible things in the last couple of years. But I think we're strong enough to get through them. We are a three-person unit and we all need each other so even if one of us is upset we must persevere for the other 2. I wrote to Anne the other week and told her to come and see you and tell you, from me, that I thought dad was the best father I could ever have hoped for. I didn't appreciate him for a long time but I do now and I'll defend him against anyone. He is a very brave dad. I still have my Valentine card on my desk and it makes me cry and I'll always remember him saying, 'If you have any trouble at all, just come straight back up here and fuck everything else.' Sorry for kicking you in the varicose veins once, dad. And all the rest.

The Geordie came to my room tonight and said, 'I've got a couple of female friends back tonight. If you're lonely come down. They're not Southerners, you'll like them.' I said I was busy writing and he said to stay in tomorrow night so he can cook my tea and we can spend the night chatting. He's really sweet (but not my type, i.e. only 21) but he comes up to my room every night no matter what time he gets back from work to ask if I'm ok.

He was all apologetic about the fact that he had a couple of friends back tonight so it stopped us having our wee talk. He's looking forward to meeting Anne next weekend as he thinks people from the north are the only people worth having anything to do with, and he doesn't know any down here except me (a fair point).

I've also made another sort of friend at work. Alva, a nice black boy (well, he's 31) who I think is gay and who has been offered another job but said he would have left Ladbrokes weeks ago if he hadn't been working with me. I asked him to give me his phone number so we can keep in touch after he leaves but, in London, even people who you get on really well with don't really want anything to do with you once they've passed out of your life (there are another ten million people to choose from). Oh well, I think I'll probably get on with the new manageress despite the fact that I was told I should resign if she was the new manageress. She talks more than anyone I've ever known but that's obviously because she's as insecure as the rest of us. She's ok anyway. She's lost 4 and a half stone in weight by having 24 Ferrero Rocher chocolates for lunch every day (I watched her eat them.) Sounds like a good diet. She's telling me about it on Friday when I work with her again.

By the way, mum. I just remembered tonight that we had a little deal. I stay in London and do my course and you stop smoking? Remember? Because you are miserable about work and things I can understand and empathise with your continuing smoking but it is very bad for you. On one hand I want you to live as long as possible and on the other I want you to be happy so I can't really pass judgement. Perhaps, instead of the smoking deal, the deal should be that you start getting Pappa's papers together to get them published.

Thanks for your letter today. I'm sorry you're miserable at work. I don't know what to suggest if you can't afford to give up work. Never mind. Mr Kinnock will be prime minister within the next 2 years and I'll become a successful writer so don't worry. I'll enclose some photos of the flat/room I'm living in at the moment so you can see what a lap of luxury I am living in. A 5-minute walk from Charles Dance's house (just a point that may impress Auntie).

I'll try and sort *your* problems out when I'm home in 4 weeks. I'm sorry you're sad. You could come down for a few days if you liked but London is so fast and nasty to those not used to it these days that I don't think it would be that therapeutic, anyway, come down if you like. I'll take you to a show and buy you a meal.

I have an extra single bed and, due to the fact that my flatmates have people unsolicited back to stay all the time, I wouldn't need to pay the £15 the landlords usually charge for friends staying overnight. Think about it.

I'll help you with your problems on the phone. Both be happy. I'm away to make some sausages and beans.

Love you both,

Your wee baby bear,

Laura xxxx

Monday, 11 March 1990

Bonny Wee Thing,

Thank you, thank you for your lovely letter which gave me mucho, mucho happiness and Dad phoned at lunchtime to say how happy it made him too. Bless your little cotton socks or big, holey woolly ones.

This is just a wee quickie note mainly to send illustrations of the sale shirts – these are on either side page 137 – E Multi, and page 138 – C Navy and white stripe. Both are size 24 and are loose fitting. I have ordered both – if you want both I will get them for your Easter. If you only like one then I can return it or if you don't like either I can return both (page from catalogue enclosed).

They should look nice with your trousers.

Feeling a bit brighter although I have buggered the computer twice in two days. It doesn't like me and I hate it.

Hope you maybe heard from you-know-who-today!![34]

Hope you enjoyed college today.

Looking forward to seeing your stories in print.

---

[34] Dennis Nilsen.

Dad and I are thinking of having another week-long cheapy trip to Yugoslavia. The *News* were advertising one from 28th April to Dubrovnik.

We could combine it as a treat for Dad's birthday and our 30th wedding anniversary. Everyone has been asking, 'Are you having a do for your anniversary?' Apart from you, I can't think of anyone we would want to have a do with, so if we go away we don't need to bother. It wasn't like our Silver when Grandma and Pappa were here. Bring you back duty-free baccy if we manage a booking.

Thanks for the photos – room looks nice. I like the art nouveau beer-can decorations.

I won't make this long. Want to catch post – thanks for giving me your pen name – you could have made it Laura Hamilton – very distinguished, but thanks for my literary immortality anyway. A great honour.

Looking forward to seeing you soon, kitten. Fondest love and kisses.

Your own Mumsie

P.S. *Dirty Rotten Scoundrels* and *Nuts* were great – you must see them.

13 March 1990

My Darling Wee Girl,

Dad is at Cam's tonight and I am on my own and have been told today I must rest and relax more. You know how difficult it is for me to relax. Remember how difficult it is for me to sit and watch a video right through.

So to force myself I will stick some superglue on my bottom and relax and write to my baby.

I am so proud at how you have managed to get yourself organised again and face a formidable task – you will make it, my love. You have guts. A few weeks ago I thought the odds were very much against you and wanted to drag you from the London train, and that first night when you arrived back in London to find the room cold and dark I wanted to scream, 'Come back little Sheba,' but you survived it.

I was listening to Marti Caine on *Terry Wogan* a little while ago. She said, 'It is not the good times in life which strengthen your life, but the bad times make you appreciate life.' She believes you can conquer anything. She has beaten cancer (hopefully) and a very unhappy childhood. If this is the case, you must be a veritable Samson.

I wish I could lick my problems. You must give me lessons in guts and single-mindedness.

All I want to do for myself now is do the job I loved really well and be a good mum and wife, but this bloody operation has ruined my memory and concentration. They have established that my memory was damaged during the operation plus my ability to concentrate for very long. I stupidly returned to work before I should have done, without completing my full physiotherapy. When I returned, everything had changed, a computer installed, work systems all changed for the new National Health changes to come into force at the end of the month. I would say,

'F*** Margaret T.' but 'you-know-who'[35] might read the letter and think your crazy mum's a 'Bolshy'. We can't have that.

My psychologist says, 'Why try so hard? Relax, relax, panic makes your memory and concentration worse, don't feel guilty if you make a mistake, don't try to please everyone around. Think more highly of yourself. Unless you do, no-one else will. You can't win everyone around. Why worry if you are not the best housewife, the best employee, the best wife, mother, sister, friend. You have come through hell and survived. Say – "I am doing my best at present. I cannot do the impossible. I believe in me." Say no sometimes. "I am tired. I must rest." When you believe in others, they will believe in you.' I hope she is right. I can't believe in me any more.

I keep a daily diary in which I show her what worried me, how I coped, how I think I should have coped. I tell her about 'my favourite doctor'. 'Ignore him,' she said.

I tell her about my sister – 'Oh, sibling rivalry is natural.' I cheat her sometimes (ha ha). I tell her I have a wonderful husband (true), who is understanding and loves me (true), and hardworking (true). I don't mention he picks his feet and snores and when I ask for opinions, says, 'whatever

---

[35] Since David's departure I'd started to notice things had been moved and disturbed in the room sometimes when I'd been out. As the landlord was the only other person with a key, I assumed it was him and would leave messages to this effect in drawers and on the desk to let him know I was on to him.

you think, my dear,' but then I don't say certain people treated him like shit because he wasn't Tommy.[36]

I tell her about the only successful, creative thing I did in my life – producing, after 6 years, a perfect, beautiful, sensitive, brilliant child. I don't tell her I was a pushy mother or that I left you to other people's tender mercies during the holidays when I worked at the job I adored. That I enjoyed exposing you to music, literature and art at an early age because it gave *me* pleasure. You may have been happier playing with dollies, trying on frilly dresses, marrying Mark[37] and having 2.5 babies, a mortgage, leaving school at 15-plus, getting a job in an office, going to discos, having a perm 3 times a year. No darling, I would not have you different to what you are – my beloved child – but I wonder if you would have been happier – but then would it have been fair to have deprived the world of you and your creative ability? Mozart wouldn't have made it if his dad, Leopold, hadn't been pushy but then Robert Burns did and his father wasn't pushy. Oh hell – shut up, June.

My psychologist loves you. She doesn't know about 'you-know-who' or David (none of her business). She loves dad (doesn't know about his feet or snoring). She loves Auntie Margaret, Uncle Jack and Nannie. She likes Ian and Uncle Jim (a bit) although she doesn't know about 'Peter Pan'. Don't want her to think I am 'nuts'. She loves Pappa, likes Grandma and thinks I am a 'wimp'.

---

[36] Mum's boyfriend prior to meeting dad.
[37] My childhood friend who used to live next door to us.

Shit, what does she know? A 38-year-old spinster who has never even been kissed, cuddled or desired or known the joy of holding a child in her womb and the infinite joy of giving birth to a beautiful, wonderful being.

She obviously has a rich daddy, votes for Margaret Thatcher and believes in the poll tax.

Psy-bloody-chology!!! (Split infinitives.) Sorry.

I will make it, as you, my darling, are trying to do. Let's fight together for our future.

What a bloody awful letter to send to you. I should tear it up.

If I don't tear it up, <u>always remember, never forget, I love you</u> a hundred million times.

I promise to write a sane Mumsie letter next time.

Your own ever-loving Mumsie (warts and all) xxxxxx

Roll on Easter

22 March 1990

Dear Wee Girl,

Just a little note on the first sunny day for weeks. You sounded a bit down in the mouth last night, after Anne had left. I felt really sorry for you but what could I do? It won't be long now until you are home for your Easter week. Make the most of the break, short as it is.

Don't forget to bring home as much bumf as you can in your two suitcases. Check for any summer things you may need over the next few weeks and bring home any washing that is needing done and I should have this done for you.

Don't forget to see that landlord about a reduction for poll tax. Let the bugger off with nothing.

I enclose a cutting out of the news re a poetry competition, they are certainly not throwing the prize money away but if you are interested Dad can get you an application form from the library.

I phoned the education department regarding the application form for next year, well 1990/1 grant. It should be available at the end of this month to middle of next month. Don't forget to remind me.

Dad has a cold and is dying of it, typical man. Kept waking me up during the night to ask if I was sleeping as his cold was keeping him awake. Nearly strangled him when he did it for the 6th time about 4 a.m. When I think of the hours I lie awake not moving in case I disturb him, as if I could. He slept through all the storms.

If there is such a thing as reincarnation, I shall ask to come back as a man or a seagull, given a choice that is.

I checked that you would be getting your travelling allowance today and they confirmed that it should be coming with your 3rd term grant. Hope you get all you asked for.

Talk about my bad memory, I discovered today that my disabled bus pass (no – bus pass is not disabled, I am) had expired in January 1990 and I have been travelling illegally free for two and a half months.

I will have to undergo another medical before I can be considered for another. I have this one because I have heart trouble and am unable to drive a car anyway, so it was quite a perk. I don't know if they will consider me now that I have had bionic surgery done. Of course, I could tell them about my impaired memory and how I would forget where I had parked my car (if I had one). The fact that I have been travelling with an out-of-date pass for three months should verify that but then they may think I am a crook cheating Lothian Transport. The shame of your old Mum doing time with your friend with the striped rugby shirt!!!

Life is pretty uneventful. A fortnightly visit to my therapist is about all I do for kicks. She always asks for you. I picture you to her as some young literary genius, with a string of young rich men longing to marry you but you are dedicated to your career. Dad is a cross between St Francis and Tom Conti. She always says, 'I would love to meet them.' Hell, she would really have me committed then. I just do it to make her job a bit more interesting. She must get fed up with bashed wives, abused children and perverts, not to mention the odd manic depressive and psychopath. Still, didn't Norman Bates do something like this? Maybe I am nuts. No love, joking, you are a wee pet and Dad is ok when he lets me sleep and stops snoring and sneezing.

Still mucking up the computer though. However it might just come to me someday before I reach retirement age.

Must go wee pet, still miss you, love you and am proud of you.

Your ever-loving, nutty Mumsie xxx

Sunday, March 31 1990

Dear Wee Girlie,

Just a quick note to send this off as promised. They don't give you much time – final captions only appeared in Friday's *News* and have to be in by Wednesday (only noticed this yesterday).

Ha! – noticed prize is trip to London to see *Aspects of Love*. Don't know if that's a prize or a punishment. Looking forward to seeing you again next Sunday. Sun is hot today.

Keep away from marching crowds in the next week and policemen on horseback with batons, or on foot with riot shields and anyone turning over cars or smashing shop windows is not doing it for exercise – run in the opposite direction.[38] What a hell of a place you chose to study – it makes the storming of the Winter Palace and the French Revolution look like the work of amateurs.

Hope you have fun with Alan. Give him my love. We have all come a long way and a lot of water has flowed under the bridge since he and I sat at the Waverley Station, tears dripping into our coffee as the London train carried you to the unknown – Dennis the menace and David, with the appetite for good literature still unknown to you plus 'all the slings and arrows of outrageous fortune' still in the quiver, awaiting your arrival at the journey's end. Had a crystal ball been at our disposal or clairvoyance been

---

[38] The poll tax riots in Trafalgar Square had taken place earlier that day and been broadcast on the news.

one of our gifts, we would have hauled you screaming from the train before you commenced that milestone in your life.

However, perhaps it is as well we do not know what is ahead. Think of all the experience of life – good, bad and horrendous – you would have missed to write about in the future.

Bring home your washing, camera, things you don't need and black top for sacrificial burning thereof, but most of all bring yourself for love and rest and Dad's soup.

As always and ever,

Your loving Mumsie xxx

Answers to caption competition –

I see 2 is Ron Brown – the Knicker Knocker

4 is Robin Cook – Scots MP against the poll tax

6 is Grand Slam Rugby Ream (The Floors o' Scotland)

7 is Gallagher – Scots golfer from Bathgate

9 is Malcolm Rifkind – the Scottish wimp

10 is Stephen Hendry – snooker champ

2 April 1990

My Dearest Laura,

Just a quickie letter. Uncle Jim sent a fiver today for you. I reckon you probably need it pretty badly, so I am sending it off to you right away, with an addressed thank-you note. Could you send it off right away?

I hope you have received the form from the grants people. I phoned them again today. They say if you want your grant (if it is granted) the form should be in now or before now so it can reach you for September. They say forms would have been sent to your college. I said, had they sent a form to you Friday? They said, 'I suppose so.' I have been going bananas about it. If you don't hear by Wednesday please let me know. I am not sure what I can do but I'll try and do something. It if arrives read it carefully and send it off soon. Lay it on thick.

I must get this off.

Fondest love,

Mumsie xxx

Sunday, 22 April 1990

Ma Dear Wee Lassie,

Well, you just phoned a few moments ago. It was lovely to have a wee chat after ironing for two days on an ironing mound which never seems to get any less but still gives me the problem of dozens of newly ironed shirts and blouses and no room in wardrobes in which to put them. It reminds me of the Labours of Hercules – however, all going well I should have a week off, no ironing, or lack of space, or feeling guilty about not doing the ironing, or filling the freezer fit to bursting, or feeling inadequate because my stupid brain won't adapt to new technology, or learning the 1001 changes in the Health Service since 1st April this year. But I will miss your telephone calls and knowing how you are. Wish you could have come with us. You would love Yugoslavia – a very poor country – which still has military service for the young but very few jobs or dole, with a crazy rate of inflation which has spiralled from 13,000 dinars to 60,000 dinars to the £1 since last year. However, you never see beggars or down-and-outs or drug addicts or drunks. The young people mostly have 3 or 4 part-time jobs to exist and everywhere in shops, banks and hotels you see portraits of Marshal Tito, their wartime leader – a truly great man but most of the population must not have been born under him.

I hope it will be as good as last year. I never think it is wise to return to the same place, lest we should ne'er recapture the first fine careless rapture. However, we are going to a different part this time and were attracted by it being another 'cheapie' – next best thing to a freebie.

In case of emergencies we are staying at the Plat Complex, Centre 1, Plat, Dubrovnik, Yugoslavia. I don't know the phone number but may have it when we get our tickets before the end of the week. I shall phone you one evening during the holiday for a wee while, if there is any night you would be out let me know this week. I am sorry I can't afford to be like Auntie Mo and phone every day. (Don't know why she goes away.)

As I am writing this, I have one eye watching Scott Fitzgerald's *Tender is the Night*. All his books have the same story – a rich guy with a mad or alcoholic wife. Just because he was a rich guy with a mad, alcoholic, suicidal wife, he always wrote books on the same theme. Please don't write *all* your books about malfunctioning families and mass murders. (Freudian slip??)

It seems ages since you were here – miss a nice dinner and Diet Coke and packets of crisps and a video to watch and not feeling guilty about the ironing mountain but most of all miss you being there with your stories and having you around. Even miss your funny little piques and little schizo turns. 'Love you, Mumsie.' 'Hate you, Mumsie. Why don't you love Tony Perkins and old tramps – fuck off.' 'Miss you.' 'I want to be alone.' However, it made life interesting and I miss you.

I saw Nigel Kennedy, the young violinist, being interviewed with Princess Anne and actor, Michael Palin. He plays the violin like an angel – the Max Bruch 'Concerto' and Vivaldi *Four Seasons* – dressed like a down-and-out, needs a shave badly, speaks ungrammatically and Princess A. looked as if he had a bad smell but in a way he reminded me of you (not the bad smell). The quotations of old Will Shakespeare sprang to mind – 'This above all to thine own self be true.' I don't understand how you go about things but I have confidence that you will find your true vocation and achieve great things. I am proud of you my little one, although I would not miss that black sweater with the white cream, grey trimmings. I am sure Nigel Kennedy would appreciate it for his next concert. Why not send it to him??

I am sure I am writing a lot of rubbish.

If you feel your money won't come through before we go, I can loan you some more. Remember Friday is D-Day.

I wish you would make it up with Alan, please – pretty please.[39] One cannot afford to lose friends. I know that.

I shall be thinking of you on Tuesday and your interview. Good luck.

Work hard in the next few weeks, little one. All the work you have done for 3rd year depends on you passing your 2nd year exams and I know you can make it. You have already had the guts to overcome tremendous odds.

Feeling a bit tired now – this is such a garbled letter. Hope it makes some sense.

Take care while we are away. You are the most precious thing in life to Dad and me. We love you always and ever.

Remember to send me a copy of your Pappa poem. I shall treasure it forever.[40]

Your ever-loving Mumsie (miss you) xxxx

xxxx

Sunday, 20 May 1990

My Dearest Wee Girlie,

Well it is Sunday. Taking it quietly, all the plans for really getting down to things flew out of the window when we sat down to watch *Terms of Endearment* and I wept my

---

[39] We had had a falling out after I had embarrassed him in front of friends when he visited me in London.

[40] 'Memories of a Grandfather' was a poem I wrote as part of the creative writing module of my degree course.

eyes out. Still I filled a Victoria Wine bag full of old letters and junk mail, tidied my books and polished the unit.

So I decided to write you a little note and return your horseshoe to bring you luck with your exams. I hope it does, my love. You will be in our thoughts.

I also enclose the wee graffiti book. Hope you enjoy some of them when you want a little break from your studies.

So glad Bob, David and your friend have been in touch. Wish you could make it up with Alan!!

I enclose the 2 best passport photos. They give you quite an enigmatic look and should be quite effective in the impression of a young and upcoming new writer.

Could you do me a favour? It is Nannie's and Auntie's birthday next Sunday. Could you post those 2 cards from London? I have written, addressed and stamped them from you, if you could just post them. They both still give you presents and there are not many people who do anymore. So if you can post them by Thursday to make sure they arrive in time.

We have had more socialising this week than we have in ages, a nice night at Anne's, afternoon at *The Mikado*, a run and afternoon tea with Margaret and Jack yesterday and an evening meal with Morag and Bob, wowee. When we came home, Carole and Pam were phoning to find out where their mum and dad were. They had been out for 2 hours without them and they were worried. Nikki has been given a chance to study Sociology in Copenhagen for a term – on a grant. I was trying to persuade Morag last night to let her go – she is 20 on her birthday but they think she is too timid to go abroad on her own. I phoned Nikki today and told her she must go to help her grow up and be more independent.

I hope with all my heart that all goes well for you in the next few weeks. Make the most of any studying time you have left. You have lost such a lot but I am sure you can still make it.

Well, I have brought some work to do this weekend. I must get on with it and the ironing mountain, if any time left.

Miss you a lot but it won't be long before you return to the civilised Scots to refresh your body, mind and soul.

Love ya, baby. Miss ya, baby, be good

As always and ever,

Your ever-loving Mumsie xx

1990, PART TWO

How Can I Be More Clever When I'm Already a Genius?

When I finally left the flat in East Finchley, I had to move all the belongings I'd taken down and accumulated since 1988, aside from a few books and clothes which the landlord let me store until I returned for my final year at polytechnic. By the time I got back down, most of what I'd left had gone missing.

It was good to be home for the summer holidays — I found some temping work, watched videos, spent afternoons with mum, went to the cinema together. My friend Anne had bought a house in Dalry by this stage where I stayed over a lot, which I hoped would mean less pressure at home as mum, dad and I weren't under each other's feet all the time and I was able to retain a bit of the freedom I was used to in London.

However, when the time arrived to go back to London, mum was upset that as she'd been back at work and I'd been staying at Anne's, we hadn't spent much time together; that I was suddenly disappearing again before we'd had a proper opportunity to talk. In retrospect, I see how I was probably using the distance of both these factors as a way to continue avoiding confronting mum's growing concerns about her memory, concentration and work. On the few occasions she had tried to discuss them I'd pathetically reacted with fear and defensiveness rather than trying to accept what was going on and to reciprocate some of the unconditional support and love she'd always sheltered and nourished me with. I was sure that the stress from my housing and relationship crises of the previous months had exacerbated her problems. I hoped if I could get through my final year at Middlesex without dropping some other emotional bombshell, it might help.

Just before going back down to start my final year, I was again offered a place at the Methodist hostel in Muswell Hill where I had originally been meant to stay when I first went down to London. Despite my earlier reservations, aside from some minor quibbles, it was a great place. I made lots of new friends, had great support and genuine affection from the couple who ran the hostel, the Clutterbucks, and found the routine, regular meals, clean bedding and having someone notice whether you were there or not reassuring, following a time of great insecurity. Mum and dad were also much happier that I was settled in somewhere they knew I would be safe. I subsequently stayed there until my second-last term at polytechnic.

August 1990

My Dearest Laura,

I suddenly realised I will never get the chance to talk with you before you go back. Sorry, I had intended that we should have a special afternoon today, but decided to lie down for 10 minutes to make me feel a bit brighter and fell sound asleep – sorry, sorry Laura. Don't seem to be able to do anything right these days, can't even open a tin of corned beef.

Enough about me. I am stuck for words for once.

If you believed (or I) I would say, 'God keep you safe when we are absent one from the other.' But I shall still pray for your safety and happiness every minute of my life. I would like to wrap you up in a shawl as I did when you were a little baby to keep you safe, but you are a young woman with your life to lead and I admire your guts for attempting to pick up the pieces of the past 6 months.

Please, please remember if it should prove too much come home to Edinburgh. We love you always.

Mum

Monday, 17 September 1990

My Dearest Wee Girl,

Today is a Monday Holiday in Edinburgh. You know – all the shops shut, nobody to phone because they are all away in their cars.

Dad and I went up to the Orwell Lodge for dinner. It

was a very pleasant autumn afternoon as we strolled through the park, scanning the canal for bluebottles lying on their backs, but I think the swans had them for lunch before we arrived.

Orwell was quiet – a few blue-rinsed elderly, well-heeled Polwarth dowagers indulging in their usual trivial verbal diarrhoea. 'Ern't the flowers oan the table livly?' 'Eh no the gel hoos wedding was here on Seterday. She left a' the floors to the Hotel.' 'Nice gel, good joab in the benk, he is a big noise en computers – good joab. They hev a new semi in Baberton and a honeymoon in Costa del something or other. The gravy's no sae nice the day.'

My, sorry, gosh, wish I could stop listening in to other folk's conversations. It is such a bad habit. It's just Dad does not talk while he is eating. What else can I do?

It was a good meal – about £6 for 2 courses for 2. Of course, my usual canny Scottish instinct was doing a mental tote of how <u>little</u> I could have made it for. I am a miserable, sorry soul about eating out and taxis. Must date back to my deprived wartime childhood.

In the Orwell there is the most beautiful stained-glass window. I have always admired it. 'Priceless it is,' said the waitress. 'The original owner had it built as a memorial to their pet whippet.' A stained-glass window for a dug! Quite spoiled my dinner it did.

We had a good weekend and a frustrating weekend. Frustrating because this guy who was going to transform our bathroom and kitchen, methinks is a bit of a ~~sh~~, sorry, charlatan.

1 He wanted to start the job before the sanction came from the grants people.

2 He said he had ordered the worktops, units and sink, without us seeing them.

3 He hasn't given us typed estimates for the kitchen and bathroom, only the lead work.

4 He asked us for a £1500 advance before he started – I just about fainted – so we are back to square 1. We had decided he had lots of good ideas and the other 6 could not care less. I wanted to have it all over by Christmas.

We had a good time at M. and J.'s golden wedding on Saturday. Yesterday we went to Nick's and Helen's house for some more wedding cake and coffee. Nick was looking for new ideas for commercials. I told him all the ads with a classical music background have been successful – right back to 'O Sole Mio' being used for Cornettos and the *New World Symphony* for dog food. *Cavalleria Rusticana* for tissue hankies. Babies and animals are always successful. He had approached Robbie Coltrane to do a commercial but he wanted a ridiculous amount of money for it. Wish someone would ask us to do a commercial.

Later we had tea again at M. & Jack's to finish off the goodies left over from the banquet the night before. To Dad's joy, we all watched the Pavarotti/Domingo/Carreras concert. M. and Jack had not seen it previously.

So we have 2 more weeks of holidays to fill in. Everyone is trying to chivvy us to go away but I want to save spare cash for the jobs needing done and I enjoy having a long lie in my own bed, no work pressures, Dad and I being able to eat together and have a pub lunch and a trip into town, catching up on little chores we never have time for.

Wish I had been off when you were here. We could have had some fun.

I miss those little afternoons we had together, our chats and videos and I loved that afternoon we had lunch and cinema. Those memories keep me going when you are away.

The Houslers are returning from the USA. Of course I will up-stage their holiday telling them how you are enjoying the hostel. How you thoroughly enjoyed your last exams and how hard you are working for Straight A (Hons) in your BA next year.

I really intended just writing a little note to enclose your cheque but I got carried away writing on this paper in all your favourite bog-roll colours.

Give my love to Bob when you see him and David, if you ever see him.

I have not dated the cheque because I am not sure when it is due.

Dad and I and Margaret and Jack are so pleased you are happy in the Hostel. It is such a weight off our minds.

Drop me one of your literary gems when you have time. I enjoy reading them.

Yer faither sends his love.

As always and ever,

Love from Mumsie xx

P.S. I just smashed accidentally that little girl toby jug which Sue gave me 15 years ago because it looked like you. I am vexed. Keep a look out for one like it in the markets on the antiques. I loved that jug.

[*Card with young girl on the front. Mum has added Doc Marten boots, messy hair and a speech bubble that says, 'Oh Mumsie, how can I be more clever when I'm already a genius?'*]

Thursday, 29 November 1990

When I was keeping my appointment with my psychologist at Astley Ainslie today, I popped in to see old Nannie. She was upset, not because she hadn't had a visitor for 3 weeks, but because she had been unable to get a card for your birthday. I felt so ashamed I stayed with her for a couple of hours and she was as high as a kite. Audrey hasn't been to see her for 8 weeks. The hospital now take her pension to pay for her keep and she still has to pay rent and poll tax on her wee house.

The hospital want her to go into a home but she does not feel old enough yet!! She hopes they will keep her until after the festive season, so that she will not be alone. And then she is going to try and make it alone again. 2 fractured femurs and 2 fractures in her arm. Struggles to dress herself, drinks milk to strengthen her bones for the first time since her mother weaned her. I have taken her lots of clothes of my own and from charity shops and she always looks very trendy. 'Laura is just like me' she says. 'Knows what she wants and lets nothing stand in her way – not afraid of hard work and knows the only way to make money and be a success is to work for it. Maybe my candles work a <u>wee</u> bit but Laura has faith in Laura and I have faith in Laura. She will make it – she has true grit like me.' With that she pressed a fiver into my hand from a sadly depleted old purse. 'Give this to her with Nannie's love for her birthday. Tell her to buy a book to make her more clever.' I didn't want to take the money but have you ever tried saying 'no' to Nannie?

So here it is posted as soon as I got home – get your book to make you clever. I hope it will be safe sending it as she gave me it. If you want to drop her a wee note she is at Millbank B Pavilion, Astley Ainslie Hospital, Grange Loan, Edinburgh.

I said I was sure you wouldn't forget her when you became 'more clever'. What a woman. We must try to visit her before Christmas when you are home – she always talks about the lovely surprise at seeing you last time. While you are waiting to visit people who have killed people, it would be nice to visit someone who is dying for a visit.[41] We are going to be busy with Dad in the Royal Infirmary but you are always a tower of strength to me.

My psychologist, Anya, sends her love to you. She has really got to know you during our sessions together.

---

[41] Dennis Nilsen had suggested in one of his letters that I visit him in prison.

Well, my love, I must dash and try to catch the post.
Hope all is well. Hope this arrives safely.
Lots of love and love and xxxs
Mumsie

1991

The Birds Will Be Building Their Nests in My Bras

During the Christmas holidays, dad was in hospital for an angioplasty procedure. Problems with high cholesterol, and a previously undetected stroke while he was still working for the brewery had led to a weakening of his coronary arteries. Although we were assured by the hospital staff that the procedure was relatively minor, the few days that dad was in hospital were extremely worrying for mum and me. The idea of a balloon being inserted and inflated near dad's heart sounded just too scary to be 'minor'. But dad, being dad, was completely undaunted by the prospect and was probably the one that calmed us down rather than the other way about. Indeed, he relished being in hospital, as he did the few times over the course of his life he was an in-patient – the guests, gifts, attention of the nurses, new people to talk to. The operation was a success and within days of dad returning home he was up and about and eager to get back to his usual routine. It was as if he'd been given a transfusion of energy and enthusiasm. We joked with him that his speedy recovery and replenished *joie de vivre* were down to the fact that he simply couldn't bear the thought of potentially missing Christmas dinner. (Especially as mum had promised to order a Chinese buffet – dad's favourite – as a treat instead of the traditional Christmas lunch.)

It was a very happy holiday. The improvement in dad's health was infectiously invigorating for us all. As I was still staying in the Methodist Hostel at the time, this also helped alleviate any added tension when I was home as mum and dad were pleased I'd settled well into somewhere secure.

In April 1991 I finally got another place in halls of residence, at my original campus in Tottenham. As my studies were still based at Enfield, and most of my friends stayed in a flat in Ponders End there, that is where I spent most of my time. During the Easter holidays several of my friends from college came up to visit and meet the woman whose letters they'd been reading for the past few years. Mum threw a party for us and a great night was had. Mum and I got on well over the holidays and as usual enjoyed watching videos together, watching *Fifteen to One* in the afternoon and the occasional disastrous shopping trip.

After a few months in halls, I was offered a room in a flat nearer the college in Edmonton. That only lasted a couple of weeks, then a room became vacant in the flat next door to my friends in Ponders End, so I moved there.

Saturday, 2 February 1991

Dearest Wee Lass,

Well it is Saturday night and I am having a lazy night as Dad is having a night at Lilo Lil's, so why should I kill myself.[42]

We had a run in the early spring sunshine to Haddington with Margaret and Jack. It would have been idyllic but I think Jonathan is going through a middle-age crisis. Margaret is convinced that all he needs is a good job (who doesn't?) and to get that all he needs is for <u>you</u> to write his CV and fill in all his application forms. Well it might work and I suppose it would pay them back for all Jack's glowing references for you and the piles of poetry books he is giving us – rare stuff – W.H. Davies, a Rupert Brooke early edition published in the trenches by the looks of it, a Kilmarnock edition of Robert Burns but no first edition of David Johnson of Melton Mowbray.

I was thinking of you a little while ago. Excerpts from *The Magic Flute* were on TV and I smiled, remembering you were the only baby in the neighbourhood who sang 'Papageno's Aria' in her pram. La la <u>la</u> la la <u>la</u> la la la <u>la</u> la la la <u>la</u> la la la la la la la <u>la</u> when the rest of them were still stuggling with 'Bla Bla Black Sheep'.

Morag is in mourning. 'The bairn is going to Denmark

---

[42] Mum used to jokingly refer to Cam, who ran the guest house in town as Lilo Lil, after the father's mistress in Carla Lane's *Bread,* which was a popular TV show at the time.

tomorrow,' she moans. She took the 8 of them, plus the 2 embryonic grandkids and little friend Julie to a hotel for a 'farewell to the bairn for 6 weeks' dinner, with never a thought for the starving millions in Cambodia, or how Kate Adie's mother feels, or how guilty I felt at sending my bairn to London for 3 years with 2 tuna rolls, a KitKat and a Diet Coke. She always makes me feel inadequate.

Dad bought himself a lovely overcoat from Oxfam in Haddington – £15 – one of his horses came romping home today. His cup overfloweth – a winner, an almost new overcoat, a night with Lilo Lil and 15 starving Asians saved with the overcoat money. It's an ill-wind. One lame horse giving happiness to 17 people. (Margaret was not happy – she thought £15 a wanton extravagance.) She bought an overcoat for herself for £1 but I hadn't the heart to tell her it was too tight, too long, lining burst and had the utility tags from the days of clothes rationing in the 1939–45 war. The moth larvae had been having a good feast on the collar but she thought it a bargain at £1. Well, maybe on the *Antiques Roadshow*. (Only fed 1 starving Asian.)

We have a wee teuchter (is that how one spells 'teuchter' or is it 'choochter?'). Never mind. He comes from Stornoway (remember Donna and Mina?[43]) and is staying for a wee while and was frightened of the big tough Welshmen here for the International. I don't mean here

---

[43] Two students from Stornoway who lodged with us when I was younger.

but in Edinburgh. 'They are so rough and wild and drunk and sing Welsh songs.' Hell, does he expect them to sing 'Scotland the Brave'? He is quite a change from the other banana boy – but every night he stays is another button on your blazer.

Well my lovely. All those crazy people. Only you and I are normal and I sometimes have doubts about us!

Talking about your blazers – illustrations enclosed.[44] Let me know if you fancy either of them. I think page 239 in black looks nice. What do you think? Fancy the jeans on 269? Let me know darling.

Must go now. Dad's home.

Love and xxxs

Mumsie

Tuesday, 16 April 1991

Dearest Wee Girlie,

Just had your phone call. So happy, happy you found a place in halls after all. There will be no stopping you (work-wise) now that you have a big room of your own with a desk. You deserve it, love, after all the difficulties you have had with accommodation over the years. I can just see you burning the midnight oil and passing brilliantly. Now that's just your 2 stone!!! to lose?? Straight As in all your subjects. Offer of a brilliant job in the Prison Service and

---

[44] Pages torn from mum's Peter Craig catalogue enclosed with the letter.

you have arrived. Can't blame me for being an optimist after all those brilliant salads you made on Saturday and you being 'the best hostess with the mostest' and the only sober one at the party and your mother being 'greeting drunk' and doesn't remember it.

The house was so quiet on Monday. I was on holiday, Dad was working. I really missed my baby at *Fifteen to One* time – couldn't bear to watch it or I would have been 'greeting sober'. Certainly, I didn't wake up until midday, made up for lost sleep on Sunday morning when I held court, must have bored your old chums senseless relating to them tales of all my yesterdays. They were very sweet, bless them. They really made the party for me, as did you.

They have a new partner at the practice. A young lad – you would like him. A cross between Dr W and the chemist.

I am sending the letter that butcher gave you in case all your teeth fall out.[45] I spat on her window as I passed her shop today.

I am also enclosing the Des article from the *News of the World*. Jack saw it. I never read the rag. Think Dad gets it for the bingo. Jack, like Ian, reads every page here, muttering, 'Tut, tut, filthy filthy, oh no, look at those boobs, make you sick.'

I am enclosing the card I bought for you to give Dad. I thought the words were lovely and appropriate. Don't

---

[45] Following root-canal treatment it took several weeks of antibiotics to clear up an ensuing infection.

forget to post it in time for the 28th April. He will only get 3 and it is his 60th birthday.

I also enclose your notebooks – and fags – there was only 1 packet in the bag. I will bring you some from Majorca and a lighter. I, of course, will be giving up after I hear you are graduating and by then you will be soo slim and I will be so fat with giving up fags. The birds will be building their nests in my bras.

Don't forget to keep some money in the bank for your poll tax. It will catch up with you and you will probably find it arrives at a time when you are broke.

It might be a good idea to inform the English Prison Service of your change of address or ask them to send any notification here and I will forward it – Saughton too. At least you are sure you will get all important mail at this particular time. I am sure a lot of your mail has gone astray in the past.

I keep laughing every time I think of Anne and that arm.[46] She was even funnier than the night she first-footed us and became entangled with the rose bush. She is a natural comedienne when she has had a few drinks.

Well love, I must close. Nearly sleepy-bye time.

T'care, work hard, have fun and try and get enough sleep.

Luv and xxxs from Mumsie

Big hug from Faither!! [*Dad's writing*]

---

[46] My friend Anne had brought a fake, dismembered arm to a party mum and dad held for my London friends while I was home.

153

16 May 1991

Dear Wee Girlie,

As Mumsie won't be around to wish you luck daily from the 25th May until the 6th June at a crucial time in your career, here is a little pussy card to look at every morning and the message from Mumsie's heart says, 'Good luck. All these warm feelings go with you today. Hope you do well.' So even if I am on some Spanish island, I am always with you, as we know miles mean nothing to you and I. We always live in one another's hearts (even if mine does tick a bit louder than yours). I send my vibrations to you my lovely. The attached £5 is to buy a couple of bottles of wine to share with your friends next Saturday 25th May. All your paperwork will be handed in by then so you can allow yourselves a night off before swotting for the exams. Wish us bon voyage or bon flying.

Also returned is your camera. 'Merci beaucoup' for the sweet thought. Enclosed a new spool for you, as interest on the loan of the camera.

Also enclosed, 2 lucky pens for the exams, a new pair of cotton socks in case you have sweaty feet during the exams, 50p voucher for a can of draught Guinness, the 2 birthday cards (which I have stamped and addressed for you and have signed inside) to arrive on Saturday 25th May – please, if you don't mind. Nannie and Morag share the same birthday. (So do Vincent Price and Peter Cushing, so much for signs of the Zodiac!!)

I will try to phone you on the first Wednesday evening at Claire's flat (I will check the number again).

If you feel you will need any cash, let me know this week.

I must finish now, love. Dad sends his love and best wishes for your success.

In case of dire emergencies, we are staying at: THE ROCADOR PLAZA HOTEL, CALA D'OR, MAJORCA – TEL: 010 3471 657075.

LUV U

Mumsie xxx

[*Message on pussy card — 'Hope you do well in the next few weeks and always. But most important be healthy and happy always. Your ever loving Mumsie, as always and forever. xxx'*]

Friday, 24 May 1991, 3 p.m.

Dearest Wee Lassie,

Well you almost made your deadline. How on earth did you manage to pull a 4-day extension for Dennis? In case you do not manage to get through tonight or fall asleep for 48 hours after your long hours and pep pills and celebration I am sending a last wee 'billy doo' before my fond *au revoir*s.

Work hard on Dennis. I am delighted your tutor commended it so highly. Please mention your correspondence c/o H.M. Prisons. I am sure it will show a lot of initiative. Do think of that book for the future. Brian Masters' is the only book on the subject and there has been lots written about Crippen, Jack the Ripper, Christie, the Moors Killers and the Yorkshire Ripper. However, that is for the future. Work hard for the exams when I am away, don't leave it for a last-minute cram, but I am sure by now you will have learned the folly of that.

Tomorrow at this time we should have reached our destination. That is if I ever get this packing finished and don't forget passports or flight tickets.

I will be glad of the rest. Was slowly grinding to a halt – dead beat but poor Laura, you must be absolutely worn out.

I enclose your student reference number in case you wanted to apply for a grant for that English teaching course. Apply for the grant form as soon as poss. It takes ages.

Dad saw the doc today. He is not referring him to a consultant, so that is a relief.

Margaret wonders if you could ring her on Wednesday evening before I ring you. Or even Thursday so that you can tell me if she has sold her house. When I phone I will only be interested in you but keep the old girl happy. I will try to phone you at Claire's on Wednesday evening sometime. So keep handy, it will be brief, so don't have them going to fetch you from the off-licence. Don't even have a 'wee-wee' after 6 p.m., even if your bladder bursts.

Morag and Bob are going to Paris at the end of June, as a wee aperitif to celebrate Bob's redundancy money, before Disneyland in the fall, as they call it. 'How super,' I said. 'You must go to Versailles, Montmartre, Sacré Coeur, Pigalle, Père Lachaise.' 'No,' she said, 'we will have a sail on the Seine,' and probably take 200 photos of the Eiffel Tower and l'Arc de Triomphe.

The £50 cheque materialised again in the account so I am returning the £50 in case of emergencies 'in absentia'.

We should return home around lunchtime on Saturday 8th June. You should be well into exams by then. Give us a ring in the afternoon if you are not too busy swotting.

You have been constantly in my thoughts during the past couple of days. Did you sense the vibrations??

Well, that's all the news, except we had a wee minister staying for the General Assembly. I was boasting about my clever daughter (whose room he was occupying) studying English Lit in London and only realised after he left that your *Good News Bible* and hymn book were lying next to your *Forum* collection on the book shelf – oh well, he can base a sermon on it when he returns to his village in Aberdeen.

Now, this isn't good enough, you know I would rather write than do housework. Must dash.

Good luck (once again), miss you, miss you, love you, love you.

Your ever-loving Mumsie

As always and ever xxxxxx

[*On envelope — Laura — Urgent — open immediately.*]

Monday, 10 June 1991

My Dearest Laura,

Just a quick note to wish you all the best in the rest of your exams. You will be constantly in my thoughts.

I am enclosing the details from Saughton. I will phone tomorrow to say you will be contacting them before the end of the week. I am enclosing a stamped envelope in case you don't have one, please write immediately, promise, explaining about your exam and asking if you could be considered to sit the exam at the next earliest date. She told me today the English prisons take ages to get in touch, if ever. So Scotland seems a better bet to start off. You can always get a transfer once you are established.

I am enclosing another £10 cash. It is not much but please don't spend it in the pub, Laura.

Sending off some of your 300 fags & lighter. Hope you like the Spanish T-shirt.

Good luck, bless you little one on the last lap of your adventure, put the final few days to good use, I am sure you will.

Dad sends his love and best wishes. We are proud of you.

Love as always & ever,
Mumsie
P.S. You have to send the letter to the Personnel Officer at Calton House.

22 July 1991

My Dearest Wee Girl,
Yesterday was my happiest day since the day you were born. I felt drunk without wine. Congratulations.[47]

This is in haste to catch post. Today's *Scotsman* enclosed plus 3 jobs from the *News* which might interest you.

I have phoned and written to some in *The Scotsman* but have marked the ones I have attended to. I have done nothing about the 3 *News* ones.

Enclosed find:

1. Book of stamps
2. Card from Mumsie & Dad. The £5 is from Dad. He worked in Lilo's last night and wanted you to have the £5 she gave him. Isn't that nice?
3. As duty-frees are finished enclosed are nearest thing in shape.

[Enclosed was a packet of mum's own duty-free cigarettes.]

Love & cuddles,
Mumsie xx

---

[47] Results of final exams were announced and I discovered I'd been awarded at 2.1 for my degree.

24 July 1991

Dear Laura,

Dad and I visited old Nannie today because we wanted to give her your good news personally. She was so happy for you, we thought she would have a heart attack with the excitement. She was crying because she could not tell you personally how happy you had made her so I agreed to write this letter with her dictating. It took an hour and a half because she kept reminiscing about what a wonderful child I had. There is something wonderful about being loved so blindly as Nannie has loved us.

The letter is exactly as she quoted it, although I changed the fiver to Bank of England. Please drop her a little note. She is rather frail and keeps all the loving thank-you notes you <u>didn't</u> send her tied with a pink ribbon and reads them over and over again.

Hope the job hunt is bearing fruit. Must go, love, it is getting late and she wants you to have this as soon as possible.

Fondest love as always,
Mumsie xxx

[*Transcript of Nannie's letter*]

Tuesday

My Darling Laura
Your Mum and Dad came to visit me today to tell me the wonderful news about you getting you honours degree.

Now I don't get out any more to buy a card, much as I would like to and even if I could still walk, I can't write any more since I broke my arm last year but I wanted so desperately to tell you personally how happy you have made me and how proud I am that my special girl (next to your Mummy) has made it and I have lived long enough to have my prayers answered. You have lots of guardian angels looking out for you.

Your Mum has agreed to write this for me with me dictating. It is the only way that I can let you know how I feel.

I never doubted for a minute that you would pass with brilliant honours. I have had faith in you since you were a little girl with your legs dangling from the piano stool playing lovely music. I used to pretend that you were my little grand-daughter, the one I never had but you loved music like I did and were a go-getter like me.

Your Pappa and Grandma would have been so proud and your Great-Granny too (the one who sang 'White Wings'). You come from a family with lots of talent but who never had opportunities.

Use your inherited God-given talents to the full advantage. The world is your oyster and you have the talent, youth, qualifications, good health and an ability to make friends plus an independent spirit. I have never for a minute had any doubts about your ability. The candles will still burn for you, dear child, as long as I am here to arrange it and even when I cannot, I hope to be another guardian angel to watch over you.

Mustn't get morbid. I have kept all your sweet letters. My favourite one was when you told me how you gave a birthday party on the £5 I sent for your birthday. Mum said Alan is coming to visit. Here is another £5 to have a party. Sorry I can't make it more. Looking forward to seeing you in August. God bless and keep my Laura safe and happy.

Your loving NANNIE xxx

[*Signed by Nannie*]

July 1991

Sunday

My Darling Wee Girl,

Just a quickie letter to get the sleeping tabs off to you. Can't find my Mimms to check whether to take one or two but will check tomorrow and let you know tomorrow night.

Looking forward to Friday and seeing you again. Keep afternoon free for Mumsie. The lad who is staying is going home for the weekend on Friday. If you want a wee rest on Friday morning you will have to kip in the boxroom for a few hours but you will have your own wee bed and room for Friday and Saturday and can play your piano and have Anne over. I am pleased about that.

I won't go on. I want you to get this before you leave. Nightie night poppet.

Your loving Mumsie

After my final exams I went home for a couple of weeks, then back down to London to the flat in Ponders End and tried to find work over the summer. As I was staying so far out of Central London though, and signing on, I was limited in how many interviews I could attend due to the price of fares and as it turned out, I was offered hardly any. Still, I remained determined to stay down there. I knew that if returned to Edinburgh and started work it would be unlikely I could ever afford to relocate to London again. I existed on an overdraft, then my Switch card until it was repossessed. In the end I sold my typewriter and most of my books to survive. I was having trouble sleeping so mum sent me some sleeping tablets which I also sold. I was then prescribed sleeping tablets by my doctor in Enfield. These were sold too. At the time I would have done anything to stay down there, even though tensions were building within the flat, and my situation was getting more desperate by the day. I told mum I had interviews coming up as an excuse to stay down there. As it was, nobody seemed interested in interviewing me, let alone employing me. I'd stopped working at Ladbrokes when I'd originally moved to Ponders End as it was too far and expensive to travel from there.

While I was in Edinburgh over the summer, I was finally invited to sit the entrance exam to be a prison officer. I failed it. IQ tests were never one of my strong points. Plus, I left the door of the prison open when I'd arrived at reception which probably didn't go in my favour either.

September 1991

Tuesday

My Dearest Laura,
I hope this week will bring you a big step nearer to the golden handshake welcoming you to a brilliant future.

I am enclosing the second-last packet of duty-free fags and the fiver I promised you for the weekend, bus fares, some grub, a haircut or whatever you want to spend a fiver on.

I am on holiday now until Monday (thank God), have felt on my last legs this week – going to see Dr W. tomorrow to see if he can come up with some ideas if he gets that smile off his face long enough. It will be a change being the patient, instead of the long-suffering receptionist, smiling politely instead of saying 'Sod off, you hypo-chondriast git.' 'A drip at the end of the nose does not constitute an emergency.' I was getting to that stage in the last few days with blinding headaches and sinusitis.

Nuff about me – did you get *The Scotsman* and some of the application forms?

By the time you get this letter I hope you have a date for your interview??? Fingers crossed, eyes crossed, vibrations, Nannie's candles and all.

How I would love to see you and have a chat. Remember to keep your £40 in a safe place in case you manage to get home for a little while and if by some remote chance this job does not materialise (heaven forbid please) I think financially it would be more viable to return to Scotland but I am hoping for your sake that your dream job is there waiting for you, after coming this far in elimination rounds. I know you have lots to offer this job. You are a hard worker, you just need your first foot on the ladder and bingo, the world is your oyster.

Must have a shower now darling. You are always in my heart and thoughts.

Dad sends his love as always.

Your ever-loving Mumsie xxx

September 1991

My Dearest Laura,

Just a wee quickie note, having an early night, going to Doc H tomorrow for some blood tests to see what's causing this exhaustion.

So very, very happy you enjoyed your interview. Margaret phoned last night to hear all the questions and said you gave all the right answers. So did Ian tonight and he does lots of interviews. Hope the interviewers thought so too. Please ring me as soon as your hear. Dad and I are really rooting for you.

Hope wee Colin is taking care of you.[48] He doesn't

---

[48] Colin was a teddy bear that Margaret left beside mum's bed when she went up to visit her in Intensive Care after the heart operation. She found him when she came to and instantly christened him her 'care bear' and, like the horseshoe, she would send him to me when I needed some luck.

look much but he is a great wee guy. He found me, I didn't find him.

Well, we had a boarder last night so here is a fiver to get some groceries for the weekend. Looking forward to seeing you soon.

Love Mumsie xxxxxx

[*Letter written on notepaper with picture of 2 goblins at the bottom. Mum has put speech marks from both of them – 'Hello Laura, I am Colin your wee toughie care bear.' 'Hi Colin, I am needing someone to take care of me.'*]

October 1991

Dear Laura,

Here are the last 40 fags as promised. They have lasted quite well, haven't they?

I am sorry there still has not been anything definite about the job. It seems such a damned waste of time. I know one should not think of 'might have beens' but I keep thinking you could be coming up for your 1st month's salary at the Open University or the Common Services one (if you had got them). I suppose there is a purpose for everything but I am afraid I can't see the purpose of having 11,000 applicants for jobs, sifting through the candidates for an exam, marking all the papers, sifting again and being unable to arrange an interview for 3 weeks. It could only happen in England. Did they know you had turned down 2 interviews in Edinburgh? I know it is not your fault and you must feel

100 times worse about it and thoroughly pissed off waiting for the mail each day.

It's a real shit when you are keen and have the ability to work and red tape stops you. You are trying to get started in a career and I am fighting to hold on to the job I have done efficiently for 15 years for another 5 years but bull-shitters say one is too old at 60 (and no pension). What about Maggie Thatcher, the Queen, Liz Taylor, all older than I am but no-one says they are 'past-it'. The problem is they still think I am 53, so I shall have to confess soon – could be sacked on the spot, so am trying to keep my secret until Christmas if poss.[49]

I shall contact the dept. of employment in Edinburgh for you tomorrow and see what we can come up with. Give it another week in London, love, and if nothing happens, make up your mind to return home. If word processing and computers is what you need to get started, you can do a couple of modules after Christmas.

London is nowhere to be if you are hard up. Nowhere is fun to be when hard up but you are safe at home, boring though it may be.

I think you should see Bob at the weekend and have him treat you nicely – give him my love, thank him for always being there when you need him.

---

[49] When mum initially applied for the job at the doctor's surgery, she knocked several years off her age to increase her chances of being interviewed. However, when she reached retirement age she had to come clean.

I skimmed a fiver off the housekeeping to get you to that interview if it turns up – last one honestly – saving for Christmas.

Your horoscope for October is good (enclosed) so perhaps brighter things are on the horizon!!! [*Horoscope from* Edinburgh Evening News *enclosed.*]

Keep your chin up. They don't know what they are missing by keeping you 'on the dole'.

Write to Woolworths, Laura. Don't bother waiting to see what happens.

Dad sends his love.

Love and kisses as always and ever,

Mumsie

P.S. Write to me and get it off your chest – everything – I can always tell when you are unhappy. 'No man is an island' as John Donne said. Tell Mumsie.

October 1991

Dear Wee Lass,
I am enclosing cheque as promised.

Train fare – £45
2 weeks' rent – £60
To help with bus fares to interviews or DHSS – £10
= £115

Hope it will help a bit. Don't forget to book your train fare before you spend it as that is your last 2 months' Bond money.

Hope things will look up soon. I worry about you down
there and miss you.
Take care, my love
Your loving Mumsie xx

In late October, with things at boiling point in the flat
after the long hot summer, I finally returned to
Edinburgh with my tail between my legs. I'd had no
luck with the few interviews I had been granted, I was
in debt, I was depressed. I packed what I had left into
the two huge cases that Margaret had bought me just
before I'd first started polytechnic and got a taxi from
Ponders End to King's Cross. I remember the taxi
driver engaging me in conversation because I was upset.
He asked me where I was going. 'Home, to Scotland,'
I told him. 'Jesus,' he said, 'I've never been out of North
London myself.'

When I got home, I applied for jobs whilst taking
any temporary office work I could get. In December,
I was offered a temporary contract to work as a clerkess
in the office at Waterstone's in Princes Street for the
Christmas period. Although I was sad not to be
employed as a bookseller, I thoroughly enjoyed the job,
had great fun with the other women in the office and
prayed they'd keep me on. It also gave me enough
money to move into a flat in Morningside Road with
my friend at the time, Linda. Sadly, the contract ended
on Christmas Eve.

1992

Nothing Is Too Hard to Share

Having become very depressed over Christmas and New Year, I was referred to a psychiatrist at the Andrew Duncan Clinic and prescribed Prozac. I tried to hide my depression from mum, who had enough on her plate, by avoiding going to visit her and dad. When I did go to visit, I was withdrawn and used to fly off the handle when mum mentioned applying for jobs. I had spent the last few months trying to find work and had only had a couple of interviews. As is the case when you are applying for jobs, the more often you are rejected, the harder it gets to fill in the page on the back of the application that asks you 'why you want this job (continue on separate sheet if necessary)'. I had lost the confidence to consider positions I might enjoy, let alone ones that looked awful. I felt useless that I was now getting knock-backs for jobs that paid less than the one at the civil engineers that I'd left to go and study and supposedly improve myself. It had been my decision to do so in the first place, and to be in this position now gave me an unbearable sense that I had failed.

The Prozac did not agree with me and only served to make me more aggressive and confused. One night, when I was alone in the flat, in desperation, I phoned all the people in my address book (most of them were out) and knocked back a bottle of paracetamol with a bottle of red wine. It was only when my flatmate's boyfriend turned up, drunk, out the blue, and came into my room to have a go at me that I came to. I spent the rest of the night vomiting into a basin at the side of my bed. When I woke up the following morning my face had turned dark purple and my tongue was black. I can't remember how I explained it to my flatmate. We were already not getting on very well. I locked myself in my room until my face returned to normal a week or so later.

When I did try to visit mum and dad I would usually spend only a very short time there as any attempt by mum to 'talk things through' I viewed as prying and inter-rogation instead of the caring and desperate need to help that it actually was. She must have been at her wits' end – already concerned about having to come clean regarding her real age at work and possibly losing her job, and now dad was becoming very forgetful and withdrawn. Mum was also looking for an extra job herself to help tide them over when dad wasn't well enough to find temporary work. But again, when mum tried to address any of these things, I would lose my temper and run off back to the flat, or else an argument would ensue which would leave us both feeling even more hurt and despondent. I was full of my own anger, guilt and denial about dad's health.

During this period, mum sent dad up to the flat to give me the following two letters.

14 January 1992

My Darling Laura,
When you were in London and I missed you oh-so much, I would write you a long letter and say all the things I probably would have been unable to say. Tonight you seem so much further than 600 miles away but I need so much to talk to you – no lectures, no advice.

This afternoon, you sat in the chair opposite me, picking nervously on that corn plaster. It was as if there was a 6-foot brick wall between us. You were my sad little girl, and I longed to hug you and say, 'Mummy will kiss it better,' but I could not. I longed to know about your session at the hospital and I ruined things by mentioning evening classes and the Civil Service.

I want you to know that I love you – always have, always will. Your little teddy says, 'I may look a little different but please love me.' I love you because you are different, not the usual run-of-the-mill stereotype. You are you. It is unfortunate that we sometimes have to compromise in order to grow up and bend a bit for a society which will not accept us 'warts and all', because unless we are very lucky or very single-minded, the only people we hurt are ourselves.

I am sure I bored you a million times telling you how I was a better actress than Liz Taylor, Sean Connery and the lot, and a better author than many but the truth was I was either too lazy or too scared to take the plunge with either, or with the lovers who wanted to take me away from Edinburgh. I settled for being safe. I am an old woman with my memories and realise I really loved the humdrum job I shall soon be leaving and the dear man I married 31 years ago was a treasure I could have searched the world over and never found such a faithful loving man. No-one could ever have loved me 'warts and all' as he has. It took you 2 or 3 Christmases ago to open my eyes to that at our Boxing Day party.

Yes, my love, I go around in cloud-cuckoo-land, playing fairy tales and realise what a bloody fake I am. I wanted to build a wall around you to protect you from hurt, not realising that you were being hurt inside the wall. Plying you with books, paints and music instead of letting you grow up naturally. I wish I could have given you brothers and sisters to share your secrets with but, alas, I had no control over that.

It is unfortunate that when we live our lives, the things we think we are doing for the best do not work out the way we hoped they would. Perhaps Shakespeare knew about this when he talked of loving too well but not too wisely.

I knew you did not have an easy time in London. I was proud of how you survived and succeeded against tremendous odds. Believe me, I know London left emotional and physical scars without you telling me. Why don't you try and speak to me about it sometime. I am shock-proof.

174

I am your Mum. It helps to talk to someone who loves you and has seen a lot of life – even if you don't love them. Nothing is too bad to share.

The world looks black at present, Laura. I know. Believe me, but stop underestimating yourself. I have a nice mirror to look at yourself in and see the real you – a beautiful face, beautiful hair (needing a cut), a brilliant mind (a bit mixed up and depressed just now) but still a hell of a lot to offer the world if you just keep plugging and <u>don't give up</u>. You are going to be a great asset to some company – they just don't know it yet.

Look out world when Laura really gets on the bandwagon.

I will try not to trouble you again. Sorry about this rabble but I felt I needed to write to you because you are my life and I shall always care and be here as long as I can, if you need me.

I enclose this cheque for £10 to put towards another Calor gas cylinder (please only use it for that). There may not be many more the way things are going at work.

Bless you little one,

Your ever-loving Mumsie xxx

[*Cheque still in envelope – uncashed.*]

17 February 1992

Dear Laura,

Do not worry. I shall not wait in again for you in the afternoon to bore you with my lack of conversation. Perhaps if I do not sparkle so much it is because I do have a lot of worries but you never say, 'How are you today, Mum?' or 'How is Dad?'

Do you think I do not bother about you or care? I would give anything to see you settled and happy. At the very least to see you motivated towards some goal. The main thing to do is look at the fields where there is the greatest demand and equip yourself with the necessary qualifications. Social work – 2 years – honours degree required, a grant available, plus perhaps housing benefit as you don't stay at home. Teacher training – one year – the same applies. There are many other courses you could find out about. You say you could not afford it. You can get Saturday or Sunday jobs. I see lots of them advertised.

If you decided against full-time training, there are lots of evening classes available – free to you.

I know this is ground we have gone over a hundred times but believe me, it is more satisfying to do something positive than to exist on 'pipe dreams'. You have great ability to work hard but you need to help fate a bit, especially nowadays. Please think about it. You could even give a few piano lessons to help you out or write some little articles for magazines or TV comments. If they publish mine with <u>one</u> year's[50]

---

[50] Mum's article 'A Wartime Childhood' about growing up in the Lawnmarket was originally published in the *Edinburgh Evening News* and *Edinburgh Then* (Archive Publications, 1989). Mum didn't realise her article had been included in the book until she borrowed it from Balgreen Library.

secondary education, a BA (Hons) in English stands a much better chance.

I have dozens of ideas for readers' letters, which I could pass on to you to put into your own words but if you think about it, you have hundreds of your own. You lived in London for 3 years – write about those days.

I used to say so often I wish I could build an ivory tower to keep you safe but even when you seemed to be safe – I blindly did not see that outside forces were poking holes in the foundations and were hurting you.

What I am trying to say, Laura, is this. Only you can set the wheels in motion. Don't get into the rut again after your years in London. Keep at it and don't give in. You will be hurt again and again, you will be disappointed and disillusioned but find your goal and go after it. You are capable of it.

I wish we could talk. Perhaps you could write to me and let me know how you feel sometimes. Even give it to me on the chin if you feel like it. I would rather be hurt than ignored. At least I'd feel like I exist.

Sorry to write all this. (No I am not sorry. It is all inside me.) I hope you will read it and perhaps apply some of the advice. I know you think I am a fussy, nagging old fool but I have worked for 37 years and know a bit about life and I remember you used to say, 'No-one with initiative needs to be unemployed.' I don't entirely agree with that, particularly as I shall be joining those ranks for the first time in my life on my birthday but I shall not get dole money or a pension (until Dad is 65) so our income will be halved from then. Apart from that, my job of 17 years is not 'just a job'. It is about 75% of my life now – my goal, my reason for getting up at 7 a.m., my reason for overcoming a hellish operation in record time. When my parents were around, I had a reason for being around and when Dad worked with Allied Brewers, I had a delight in decorating the house and keeping the wheels turning, but now he has withdrawn into himself, hardly speaks, falls over a lot and hurts himself. This morning he asked if I had sent the fax messages off on Friday. When I asked what he meant he said, 'I don't know. I thought you were someone else.'

This afternoon I wanted to talk all those things over with you. I was scared and worried and didn't want to go to work and leave him. The doctor referred him to a specialist but they said to leave well alone just now.

I am perhaps mad making a large hole in our savings to take him to Cyprus and the Holy Land but I need one last chance to be alone with him, in new surroundings, to devote 24 hours a day to him away from worries and stress, in the sunshine, in the Holy Land and say a little prayer for him and for you and if there is a God who listens, who knows?? You will note that I have made a point of being away on my dreaded 60th birthday. Probably I am being a bit unrealistic but I will have 2 weeks' 'pipe dreams' before facing up to the fact that the demand for 60-year-olds with dicky hearts is extremely limited. My working life is almost over (and don't you dare tell anyone I am 60, just in case it isn't) but yours is ahead of you. Use it wisely and may your working life bring you the joy and satisfaction mine did.

I am sorry it never seems to work out for you and me, when you wanted to leave home both times I did not try to hold you back, hoping that by letting you go, you would realise how much I loved you, but when you love someone, you never stop caring or worrying about them. It is not being nosy or checking up on you all the time. You just want to know they are well and happy. I had hoped we would have some time to get to know one another. To visit you in your little flat and bring Dad up to see it. He would have loved that. He asked me a lot about it. I would have loved to go out for a coffee with you like we did one day a few years ago, or go to the cinema or just chat like friends, not strangers. I obviously went very wrong somewhere along the line. Even if you could tell me where I went wrong.

Dad and I watched the tape of *Pavarotti in the Park* for the first time. I am sure we saw you 3 times. At least we think we did. I remember how you phoned me that night, so happy and excited – my girl – my real girl. The one playing the 'Intermezzo' from *Cavalleria Rusticana* – Pappa's favourite. I skipped school aged 12 and did without lunch for a week to attend a Wednesday matinee and cried the whole time. I had something to share with my Dad and we both cried every time it was played. I would love to have been in Hyde Park with you in the rain that day.

I am attaching my most treasured possession to this letter. The lucky horseshoe which you gave me before my op and I returned afterwards to help you pass your exams and you returned after you had passed. You may just need a little luck again to get you on the right path. You can always return it <u>when</u>, not <u>if</u>, you are settled in a happy career or path to one. As you know, you have to give the lucky horseshoe a bit of help. It can't do it all for you but it helps.

Must dry up now. Pavarotti singing *Tosca*. Dad just saw you again in the rain. Always here if or when you need me.

Love Mumsie

[*Horseshoe returned to mum but imprint of it still on letter.*]

1992–1997

10,000 Questions

Mum and dad made their trip to the Holy Land. They visited Cyprus then travelled to Bethlehem and Jerusalem, visiting the Wailing Wall. It had always been one of mum's dreams to travel there, as was visiting Austria, Bulgaria, Majorca (where her beloved Chopin once lived) – which they happily managed to do, despite only really starting to travel later in life.

The Prozac I had been prescribed was having an increasingly bizarre and negative effect on my mental state which culminated in me having to leave the flat in Morningside Road and move back to mum and dad's. By this time I was feeling so vulnerable, I was able to appreciate their love and support. Mum and dad were glad to have me home, and along with counselling I was lucky enough to get a place in the Day Unit at the Andrew Duncan Clinic. Having a routine again, new people to engage with and care about, activities to occupy my mind and bring me slowly out of my shell again were invaluable. Through the counselling I ironed out several issues that had troubled me for years.

With my confidence returning I was able to apply for jobs again. A week before being discharged from the Day Unit I went for an interview for the post of administrative assistant with the Scottish Prison Officers' Association (SPOA). To my enormous surprise I was offered the job on the spot. I was later told this was because I was the most nervous interviewee they had ever encountered and they felt sorry for me and wanted to see my reaction if they offered it to me. But it was a job. Finally, a full-time job. I was unable to attend my graduation as it took place only two weeks into the new job, but finally being settled felt better than any ceremony.

In the same month, August 1992, mum started working part-time as a dinner lady at George Watson's College. Each day she would bring home samples of the goodies to show us what they fed them in private schools – wild mushroom soup, ham and cream-cheese swirls. As her own mother had been a dinner lady at one point, despite the hard, physical work, mum enjoyed being in her mother's shoes in this intriguing environment and working with a diverse group of people again.

Cruelly though, just prior to her starting the new job, mum's friend, Margaret, was admitted to hospital suffering from breathing difficulties. She died at the end of mum's first week at the new job. We were bereft and devastated for Margaret's husband, Jack, who absolutely adored her (as we all did). Between subsequent bouts in hospital himself over the following months, Jack continued to take mum and dad out for runs, as they'd always done together, but everywhere they went they were invariably reminded of how much they all missed Margaret and what a huge gap she had left in all our lives. Christmas was a miserable time, without mum on the phone to Margaret most of the day. We invited Jack over to spend New Year with us, to try and raise our collective spirits in a celebration of Margaret's life. Mum started to buy in all Jack's favourite titbits. Sadly, Jack himself died of heart failure on 30 December before he was able to indulge in any of them. Margaret and Jack's ashes were scattered together under a tree in the Pentland Hills (of which Jack was laird) close to where we had all spent so many happy times at the cottage.

While mum was still reeling from losing her two dearest friends, her long-time heroine and candle-lighter, Nannie, finally went to meet her maker, aged 97, less than a month later. She died at home, as she had wished to. For years she had been saving money for drink for the send-off she'd always planned – adamant that no-one should shed a tear and everyone should have a good time. She even recorded a speech which was played at the reception after the service, thanking everyone for turning up and telling them how special they all were to her. I very much regret now not attending Nannie's funeral. She was a wonderful, inspiring lady who loved me in spite of everything.

However, as I'd already had time off for two funerals in the first month of my new job, I could not get further leave to attend.

Mum continued to work as a dinner lady at Watson's until June 1993 when she had to officially retire. At this point she also had to leave her beloved job at Polwarth Medical Practice. Having knocked six years off her age when she first applied for the job, time had finally caught up with her and she had to come clean, and consequently retire from there too. The job at the surgery had been her working life. Rather than give up though, she first took a job at Napiers herbalists, then with a couple in Morningside, the Wilsons, where she did odd-jobs, helped archive family letters and books and made two great new friends in Mr and Mrs Wilson. As the Wilsons' house is on the 38 bus route that runs past our door, dad used to chum her to work and go up to meet her when she finished in the afternoons.

Settled in my new job at the SPOA, I was soon able to ease the pressure and give them a break by moving into a room in a flat in Haymarket Terrace. This time, the distance worked well. I appreciated mum and dad a lot more being finally settled in a place nearby (but far enough to give me the feeling of my own space, with people still around, a feeling which had evaded me since my return from London).

Both suffering increasingly from ill health, mum and dad started to make the most of their time, as far as they were able. More holidays abroad, twice to Bulgaria, in 1994 and 1995, where they would get various herbal remedies for dad cheaply, plus spoil themselves with massages, aromatherapy and various treatments on Bulgaria's diverse nationalised health service. Mum kept diaries during their trips to Bulgaria for me to read when they got back, and so we had a lasting memory of these precious times. It was as if the distance, just as when I'd been in London, gave her an opportunity and space to take time to express herself again.

By 1995 dad began frequently to have falls in the street which he'd try to hide from mum to save her extra worry but would occasionally phone and confide in me about. When he finally agreed to see a doctor, various tests revealed that he'd suffered two strokes – the one previously mentioned which he'd suffered whilst still working at the brewery and another more recently. These had caused a narrowing of the arteries in the brain (cerebral arteriosclerosis). This caused increasing loss of memory, judgement and balance. His cholesterol was sky high. He had to cut back on the sweeties and cakes he loved best (dad wasn't a drinker and smoked his last cigarette in the early 1970s). But still he managed to walk every day down to his beloved Gorgie, where he had grown up.

In 1996 I took out a mortgage on a flat with my then partner, Alec, in Gorgie itself so dad was able to visit during his trips down the road. He got on well with Alec. They liked to joke about the football (dad was an avid Hearts supporter, Alec Raith Rovers and Celtic) and exchange notes on the horses. (Dad had always enjoyed a small flutter on the horses – nothing major – 5p each way – and always with horses with names that related to mum or me – operas – musicals – actresses.) Dad would even pop round to see Alec on his own, but would always keep his jacket on and only stay a short time, eager not to intrude. Now that I was working and had my own place, I used to give dad £5 pocket money to supplement the £5 pocket money mum had always given him.

Settled in the new flat, I had started writing short stories, had one published in Kevin Williamson's magazine, *Rebel Inc.* and had begun reading at various events based around the magazine. When Canongate Books offered Kevin the chance to publish Rebel Inc. books under an imprint, he commissioned my first short-story collection, *Nail and Other Stories*, along with a couple of novellas and subsequently my first novel, *Born Free*. Mum and dad were delighted – mum because I was finally managing to fulfil the creative path she had always dreamt of for me, and dad because he was proud and happy I was doing something that I loved which made mum so happy. In 1997 I was awarded a Scottish Arts Council bursary to allow me to spend time off work to concentrate on the novel, so was able to stop working at the SPOA and work full-time on writing.

Dad's health continued to deteriorate. Mum tried to talk to me about it but still I was unable to comprehend that my dad was really ill. It had always been mum who had suffered from ill health. I saw that he was more absent-minded and sometimes off in his own thoughts but he had always been a quiet man. Joking and laughter would still bring him out of his shell, as it always had. I could not acknowledge that he had changed.

Desperate for another holiday abroad together mum found she was no longer able to get holiday insurance for either of them. It was as if they were suddenly cut off from the possibility of ever again visiting the outside world. Determined not to be restricted in this way, mum booked a holiday for them both in the place we had spent so many happy holidays when I was a child – Blackpool.

Unfortunately, they also decided to use the same mode of transport that they did all those years before – the coach. On arrival they were both exhausted. Mum's ankles were filled with fluid and following another dizzy spell and fall dad ended up in hospital. It was a fortnight before he was released. As their accommodation was only booked for three days, mum had to traipse to and from the hospital whilst trying to find an alternative place to stay, move the luggage on her own, etc. I offered to go down but mum kept hoping dad would be discharged without notice and was concerned about me finding accommodation (in reality, she probably knew I would be hopeless in terms of support and we would probably end up arguing and making a bad situation even worse). It was a terrible way for them to spend their final holiday together. Eventually, when dad was released, my auntie repeated a rescue mission which she had previously done when mum had taken ill with pleurisy the last time we'd been in Blackpool in my youth, and drove down there to pick them up.

Dad was weaker when he got back but continued to make it down to Gorgie every day to have a flutter on the horses and a quick coffee with Alec or myself. Since I'd started working at the SPOA I'd been buying dad tickets to see his beloved Hearts for birthdays and Christmases as he hadn't been able to afford to go since I was a child. The manager of Alec's and my former local pub was a Hearts season ticket holder who, through work, was often unable to use his ticket and kindly said we could use it any time it was available. I told dad I would borrow it for the forthcoming Hearts v Celtic match. Alec was getting ready to go away on a fishing trip though, and I completely forgot. When dad turned up at the flat to ask about it I had to tell him I hadn't had time. He was as affable as ever, but didn't stop for a coffee as he knew I was busy writing my book.

When Alec left for his trip the following Monday it was the first night I had spent in our new house on my own. I'd always had a fear of being alone in an empty house. Everywhere I'd lived before had been with other people, in communal flats, mum and dad's, Methodist hostel, halls of residence. I sat up late working on my book, scared to finally put the light out. When I did I couldn't sleep. I lay, waiting for the sound people always dread suddenly hearing in the middle of the night, never sure what that sound will be.

At around 3.30 a.m. the phone started ringing. I dreaded picking it up to some silent caller who might be standing in the phone box across the street. When I did pick it up, I heard chaos. Mum was crying, there were people talking loudly in the background and a lot of commotion. 'It's dad,' she said. 'My darling. It's your darling daddy.' Dad had collapsed in the house. The paramedics were there. I told her I'd come up (about a fifteen-minute walk) but the paramedics had already been there some time and were about to take him up to the hospital. I heard them trying to restart his heart in the background with electric shocks. I grabbed some clothes and tried to phone a taxi. No answer. I ran out into the empty streets, frantic, and ended up running all the way to the Royal Infirmary.

I arrived in Accident and Emergency about fifteen minutes before the ambulance did. The pay-phone was broken so I couldn't phone the house again. All the staff were able to tell me was that the ambulance was on its way.

When they did arrive, I was escorted into a room with mum while they attached dad to various monitors and breathing equipment. Mum explained to me, through her anguish, that dad and she had gone to bed early and shared some chocolates. She'd woken up a few hours later to find dad wasn't there. Going through to the living room she found him sitting in his chair, crying. She comforted him and asked if he wanted some toast and tea. He seemed to perk up. Mum went through to the kitchen to get the toaster and kettle on. When she went back through to see him seconds later, he'd collapsed onto the floor. Trying desperately to get him onto his back to give him mouth-to-mouth, she was simply not strong enough to move him. After doing the best she could, she called an ambulance. Aileen, a neighbour from across the road, had noticed the ambulance outside the door and had gone over to comfort mum. Her husband had died of a heart attack years earlier when he was only in his thirties. The paramedics had managed, after twenty-five or so minutes, to get dad's heart beating again. The rest was up to Nannie's angels.

We were led through to a room where dad was attached to all sorts of cables and machines. We talked to him through the night and the next day, watching his heartbeat flutter on the monitor from slow to very slow. At several points we convinced ourselves that he'd managed to give our hands a slight squeeze. But he never regained consciousness and at three o'clock that afternoon, he died with us both at his side.

I was stunned. I didn't know what to say to mum. We hugged each other but I was suddenly caught up in a grief that I'd never known. I could not believe he was gone. Mum was the one who had always suffered from ill health. Why had I not listened to her when she'd wanted to talk to me about him being ill? Why had I never asked him the 10,000 questions that were suddenly flooding my mind that I could never now hear his honest responses to? Why had I been too lazy and self-centred to get him that season ticket for the Hearts game? Why had I never asked him why we hadn't spoken to his brother's family who had lived down in Gorgie, so close to us, for so many years? Why had I only told him I loved him when I was apologising for some way that I'd hurt him? Why had I not cherished him? Why had mum not been more insistent in telling me how unwell he was? Why hadn't she prepared me for this? Wicked, negative thoughts.

I do not think I stayed in the house with mum that night. The days after dad's death were a blur. I suspect someone else had to give her the true support she needed. But together we went through the surreal madness of organising the funeral. My uncle drove us to register the death, to the undertakers, to meet the minister, to his own house to choose what music should be played.

Despairing that my dad was going to be seen off with a speech about him by someone who had never really known him, music he hadn't helped pick himself and arguments over who went in which car, I decided I'd like to write something myself to read at the funeral. It seemed to bring mum and me together when I told her my plan.

On the day of the funeral it was arranged that dad should first be brought to our house for the last time, where mum, Morag and Bob, Alec, Ian and Jonathan would be picked up, then driven down to Gorgie for a one-minute silence outside his beloved Tynecastle football ground before proceeding to Mortonhall where the cremation was to take place.

I managed to read the speech that I had written without breaking down. I was doing it for dad, mum and me. I wanted to acknowledge, finally, the wonderful man that my dad was, even though I knew it was too late. The speech went as follows:

I just want to say a few words about dad to try and give my own impression of him. Dad gave love, support, encouragement, enthusiasm, humour but never asked for anything in return. The only time he asked me to do anything for him was in relation to mum. He'd call and remind me to phone and ask how she'd got on at the doctor's, or hospital, or dentist, or a couple of weeks ago he phoned me up and said, 'Don't get mum flowers this Sunday, she doesn't like them because they don't last. Get her carrot cake. She likes that.' He lived for us, not for himself. Mum would always chum him to the doctor's because otherwise he'd just tell them he was fine because he didn't want to take up their time.

When the doctors first discovered the cerebral arteriosclerosis, or when he had a bad turn he just seemed to ignore it. He'd always just say, 'Aye, I'm fine' or 'Don't worry about me, I'm just great.' He continued doing all the things he'd always liked doing, retained his unique and steadfast sense of humour and never complained.

No matter what life threw at him dad always kept that sense of humour. Like myself, when things upset him he either withdrew until the threat or upset had passed or tried to lighten things up with humour, and keep laughing despite everything. That is what I will remember most about dad; his laughter: whether a deadly one-liner from the man who'd been sitting demurely in the corner of the room for most of the party; or his hysterics at the banter between his visitors when he was in hospital; or gentle ribbing about his precious Hearts with friends who supported rival teams; or sometimes quite simply as the only real alternative to crying. They say that laughter is the best medicine. I just felt that as long as I could keep dad laughing he would be all right.

Everyone will have their own memories of Ronnie, but I just want to share a few I have of him as a dad: of him saving up a little of his £5 pocket money each week to buy me a top I liked a few months ago; of always insisting on bringing down any mail that arrived at Ashley Terrace for me just so he could pop in for a little chat; him sleeping in the box room and letting me share mum's bed when I was young because I was scared to be on my own; taking me up to Colinton Dell for walks every weekend when I was wee; buying me a fishing rod and trying to teach me how to fish even though he didn't know how himself; him coming through when I was going to bed each night and sitting with me by the two-bar electric fire in the bedroom, pretending we were at scout camp, singing 'Two Little Boys', 'There Was a Soldier, a Scottish Soldier'.

Material things didn't matter to dad, as long as mum and I were comfortable and safe and could have the things we needed and wanted. He just liked his hair to look nice and to always be smartly dressed. Because he never had much money of his own, he learned to be happy without it. He used to love having his little bets on the horses. The amounts he gambled were so small that the return could never be that good but he loved to buy mum and me things when he won. If I ever offered to check the results on Ceefax for him he wouldn't let me as it was having the excitement of the result to look forward to the next day that he liked best. I hope all the horses that have died over the years in the Grand National are running races in heaven for him.

As has been said quite a lot over the past few days, mum would have had to handcuff dad to the radiator before she went to work in the mornings to keep him in. I chose 'Morning Has Broken' as one of the hymns to celebrate this side of my dad. The side that couldn't wait to start the day. The side that stood on the path waiting when people were coming to visit, or would go down to the bus stop to meet mum because he couldn't wait till she got back to see her.

On days mum and dad were doing something special, dad used to be up at the crack of dawn, washed with his best clothes on, champing at the bit for it all to begin. Even after he retired he would be up at seven every morning, washed, dressed, mum's breakfast on, impatient to start the day. If you tried to contact him on the phone after he'd done the wee chores mum asked him to do while she was at work in the mornings, he would never be in. He was always out, walking about his beloved Gorgie, doing his own thing, having his wee bit of freedom. We even discovered recently he'd been popping up for a coffee with Alec when mum and I were at work and that one day my friend Alan had popped in to see mum and dad, mum was at work so dad invited him in and they shared a bottle of Martini together, though dad wasn't really a drinker. I think because dad spent the majority of his life around women and because his father died a month before he was born, he really enjoyed the rare occasions when he could have the one-to-one company of men. Alec and his brother took him to the football recently and he was completely in his element, cheering with the crowd, getting annoyed with the referee's decisions. I don't imagine Alec and Alan are the only two people he had secret little friendships with. I wonder if there are people in Gorgie at the moment with the kettle on, wondering where he's got to.

If anything needed delivered, or someone was poorly, or mum needed chummed somewhere he would always jump at the chance to get out and about and feel he was helping someone. Dad would do his best for anyone, no matter what they thought of him.

He used to love to paint and draw when I was younger and as you probably all know, at one time had one of his works hanging in the National Gallery on Princes Street. It was a poster of Santa Claus he painted for my grandfather's office at Christmas when he was the jannie there but I'm still sure it could have led to greater things.

He loved reading as well, which I think I've picked up from him. When he and mum were round at the flat for dinner a few weeks ago he kept pulling books out of the shelves and saying, 'Have you read this one, oh, that's a super one, oh, is that the one they did the film of? Is that the one about the Glasgow razor gangs?' He left with a big bag to read. He always had a couple of books on the go at the same time and loved going to the library and coming back with a big bag of books he'd picked for mum and him.

Lastly, I feel I must mention the other great passion which I had in common with him — his love of food. Dad loved going out for meals, or having a big family meal, or going round to Ian and Alan's with May and Bobbie for a wee drink and a good conversation and all the lovely wee titbits he got at Ian's that he didn't get anywhere else. The last time he was in hospital, people gave him so many sweeties that we all used to help ourselves when we were up. In the end I discovered he was hiding the bulk of his chocolates at the back of his locker and only handing out the boilings and Liquorice Allsorts when the visitors were round. When anybody used to give him sweeties as a present, he would open the bag they were in, wide-eyed, and say 'Wow wow wee!'

It's impossible to try and sum dad up in so few words but as I said I just wanted to share a few of my memories with you. All I really wanted to say was that it was a privilege to have such a kind and gentle man as a friend and father and a privilege to have known him and I hope that he's now in a kinder, happier place and reunited with all his friends and family. Thank you all for coming, and thank you for listening.

1997–1999

No Best Time of Day

Following the reception in a local hotel after dad's funeral, the strength that mum had found from somewhere to keep going since his death seemed to run out and she was hospitalised that night, and for the next six days. This was the first of seven stays in the Royal Infirmary over the next couple of years, the longest being for fifty-seven days.

During their lives together, dad had always been a faithful visitor when mum was in hospital – the visitor who was always there, who'd go up twice a day whenever possible, who stayed for the whole visiting hour and still didn't want to leave. Now she was spending so much time in hospital and he was no longer there. A lot of mum's friends from over the years rallied round – some I had heard her talking about but had never had the chance to meet. They formed a bond around mum, visited her when she was ill, and met up for lunches and nights at each other's houses when she was back home. The Golden Girls were born.

But despite the warmth and love around her, mum longed for my dad. When she was home she had to sit in the room where her beloved had faded in front of her. She began sleeping in the front room of the house as she could no longer bear to be in the bed from which he had left her for the last time. But she kept her spirit and humour up as best she could – as she always had.

Some months after dad's death, when mum was strong enough, Jonathan drove mum and me out to his family graveyard in the Pentland Hills where we planted a rowan tree, and placed dad's ashes underneath it, so we would always have a place we could come and feel near to him, and where we would both join him one day.

Through the various carers now visiting mum in the house, she was put in touch with Fiona Harkness, the District Nurse from St Columba's Hospice. I was horrified when she first mentioned the word 'hospice' to me, having always classed them as places where people went to die. But Fiona explained that mum would only be attending the Day Unit of the hospice, where she could take part in activities, meet some new people in a safe environment that she could be driven to and picked up from. I visited the hospice with mum and my preconceptions were broken. Everyone seemed lovely, welcoming, down-to-earth and immediately started to take to mum. She began attending the Day Unit early in 1999.

She seemed to thrive in the new environment; she soon made great friends with everybody, loved to tell me about them and introduced me to them all. Her confidence returned to the extent that she was able to go for a short break to Canterbury with her friend, Val (one of the Golden Girls), taking her around in the wheelchair. Despite it being her first holiday without dad since they were married, she had a wonderful time and took lots of photos and was delighted to have fresh stories and anecdotes to tell me when she got back.

The journey took its toll though, and mum had another long spell in hospital on her return. When she got out she was confined to bed with oxygen at her side. She hated the lack of independence. Her friend Gwen would take her out for lunch and runs down to Peebles Hydro (where mum and dad had gone on their honeymoon) with the oxygen tank on the back seat of the car when she felt strong enough, but she was getting gradually weaker by the day.

My last day out with mum, outwith the hospice, was early in June 1999. Mum wanted new curtains for the front room that she now spent all her time in, to brighten it up. Abandoning the oxygen she ordered us a taxi up to Jeffreys at Tollcross and asked me to help her pick curtains that we both liked. We eventually agreed on a pair of beautiful gold curtains with Latin script. Mum arranged to have them specially lined. Exhausted and ill having been off the oxygen, she then insisted on going into her favourite food shop, the Iceland store next door, to pick up some bargains and then we ordered a taxi back home.

The night before mum went into the hospice full time (10 June 1999), she threw a party for the Golden Girls at the house. They drank champagne and talked about the old days, the Palais de Danse etc. I was invited to join them but didn't go as I felt that I had let mum down. Maybe if I'd moved back up to the house and looked after her, she could have stayed there longer. I would go up to visit, cook for her when I was there and had over the past few months been helping her have a bath (something that made us both feel very close) but I was busy making final corrections to my novel (which she encouraged me to do) at the time and was in my usual state of denial.

Also, as delighted as I was that mum had a devoted group of friends around her, I felt, for the first time in my life, that I had to compete for her affection. It was the last thing I should have been worrying about but you can't help the way you respond to things. Often, prior to her becoming an in-patient at the hospice, I'd go up to the flat to make her lunch or dinner, and find one of her friends already there, cooking. For the first time, I was the one who wanted to talk, but often we would not have the privacy to do so. I can only offer my humblest apologies and thanks to the friends concerned.

Mum dived enthusiastically into her new life at the hospice. The safe freedom it allowed agreed with her. Once again she was able to attend various classes – cooking (pizza and pakora that she would proudly present me with when I visited), designing cards, stained-glass work on paper, meditation, relaxation. She derived great pleasure from taking all her guests to the hospice snack bar and insisting on filling them with sandwiches and crisps. She even purchased a painting from the exhibition showing there. She loved me taking her for a spin in the wheelchair round the hospice grounds, looking onto the Firth of Forth.

During these moments, mum started to try to talk to me about the fact that she was not going to be around for much longer. I couldn't bear to talk about such things. I could not let myself believe this was the truth. I did not want to spend this precious time with her talking about when she was not going to be there. Mum asked if I'd be willing to have some counselling with her at the hospice. She wanted to iron out any unresolved issues that she knew would eat away at me once she was gone; to prepare me for her not being there any more; to talk about how we both felt about dad.

The counselling took the form of both individual and joint sessions. In the sessions alone with the counsellor I talked about the negative whirlwind of feelings I had about dad's death, my inability to accept how ill mum now was and my anger at myself over the way I'd taken them both for granted throughout the course of my life. Through talking about these feelings, then going over them again in counselling with mum and finding out how she felt about them, I was able to let some of the anger go, to admit that a great deal of it was based on my own guilt, and to let go of some of that guilt too. I talked about all the times I had hurt them both over the years, and how hard I found that to deal with, and that despite being able to acknowledge this, I still had the capacity to be hurtful and selfish with mum. Mum said that none of it mattered, that she was my mother and she loved me whatever I did or said and knew it was because I loved them so much that I behaved the way I had. And we talked about all the good times: the operas, musicals and shows we'd seen together when I was still her wee girl and best friend; the rare shopping trips (laughing about how bloody grouchy I always was); the holidays and runs and parties at the cottage with Margaret and Jack; anecdotes about Nannie and the family. We talked about how we both felt about the family. We covered a lot of ground in a few counselling sessions. And we talked about how much mum needed me to come to terms with how little time we had left together, and her desire to see that I was settled and ready for her leaving me.

The counsellor suggested I make a tape of music for mum to listen to. I jumped at the task, compiling a tape of songs that had meaning to us both over the years, along with ABBA (whose music she was subjected to throughout the '70s), songs from *The King and I*, *Carousel*, all our favourites. When I next visited mum she'd been listening to it avidly. She told me her favourite new one was the 'I Believe in April' song – ABBA's, 'I Have a Dream'. Ironically, the real words are 'I believe in angels'.

The great friendships that mum developed with the staff, other patients and their families in the hospice and the support and love they had for each other was inspirational. Despite my misconceptions, I couldn't remember ever having been in such a life-affirming place. I offered to run a stall at the Hospice Fundraising Day in Charlotte Square. Again, the spirit of the people who organised and attended the day inspired and uplifted me. Mum was really proud that I'd taken part and couldn't wait to hear all about it when I visited her later that day.

I took mum a proof of the first four chapters of my forthcoming novel. She showed them to everyone. 'Did I tell you my daughter is a writer?' We celebrated her sixty-seventh birthday with everyone in mum's room eating Marks & Spencer cocktail sausages, sausage rolls, mini Scotch eggs and a teddy bear birthday cake (mum had a passion for teddy bears). Mum loved it when I visited after one of the cooking days and would always have a little plate of what she'd made that day for me, asking me on every bite how much I was enjoying it. 'Your mummy's still a good cook, eh?'

Other times, things weren't so good. On several occasions when I visited, I'd overreact, or become upset by something mum or one of her guests had said and would only stay for minutes. My misguided possessiveness deepened daily. When mum was no longer well enough for joint counselling I would see the counsellor on my own but was too ashamed to admit to these feelings of jealousy. As the doses of morphine mum was given increased, I became very upset when people argued over the bed as if she was already gone. I wanted to protect her from it. I wanted her all to myself.

My feelings of jealousy greatly intensified after Fiona asked if she could have a word with me during one of my visits. She explained as sensitively as she could to me that mum was not expected to live for more than a fortnight. It was so stark. It was inconceivable. Mum had always been a fighter. I knew she would keep on fighting. They didn't know her like I did. They didn't know what that bright Lawnmarket spirit was capable of.

The doses of morphine continued to increase. Mum said she wanted to say goodbye to her friends and family one last time, as she wanted them to remember her as she was. People came up over the coming days to say *au revoir* and then mum said she wanted to spend the rest of her time with me.

My partner Alec and I stayed up at the hospice, he sleeping in a side-room and me beside mum. I did not want to leave her side. I did not want to ever have to let go of her hand again. During the days I learned how it must have felt for mum all those times she'd been in hospital over the years, waiting for the visiting hour, waiting for someone to come round with a cup of tea. Desperate for some form of human contact.

At night, I would lie awake on the bed the staff put by her bed for me, and watch her sleeping, just like she had done when I was born. Over the days our roles seemed to reverse. I was beside her as she reached the end of her life, just as she had introduced me to mine. She would communicate by squeezing my hand, I would sing to her and talk about our lives and tell her what was going on in the room around us. 'I believe in April.' When I did sleep I would wake up in a panic until I was sure she was still breathing, again, just like she'd told me she had done when I was a baby. I would watch as her heart monitor would slow down and almost stop, then I would tell her I loved her and her heartbeat would speed up again. I still convinced myself she was going to come back. At one point, during the last hours of her life, when I told her I loved her I swear she whispered, 'I should think so too.' Or at least I think she did. Every movement or flutter of the monitor was filled with significance.

My darling mum died in my arms at 12.45 p.m. on 7 August 1999.

I have never been a religious person, but I had a very strong sense of her spirit having left her body. As I embraced the beautiful shell that my mum used to live in I felt a certainty that the essence of who she really was had not died, but gone somewhere else. It was as if, like Tinker Bell, she'd waved her wand and transferred herself somewhere safe from any pain, hurt, trouble or worry forever. Hopefully somewhere she would meet dad, Nannie, Margaret, Jack and her own parents and grandmother again.

A couple of days after mum's funeral, I returned to

the hospice to pick up some of her belongings – her toilet bag, smelling of her favourite Crabtree & Evelyn Lily of the Valley talc, her soap, her face cloth, her dressing gown, her handbag full of notes and mementos and photos she'd taken in with her. I found a letter which had been left for me. The letter was undated but appears to have been written at least a year before mum died. I do not know the circumstances in which she wrote it – whether in the house alone, whilst in hospital, at some unspeakable low point. It tortures me not to know; to once again not have been there for her when she felt so desperate. All I do know for sure is that it was the last letter I ever received from mum. I can only hope that by the time I discovered it, her wish had come true and that she had finally been reunited with dad. She had marked the envelope 'Private and Personal. From June A. Hird to Laura Hird.' It had already been opened.

My Darling Wee Girl,
Sorry pet, I cannot go on any longer without my darling sweetheart, your lovely Daddy, Ron. He was the most gentle, sweet, loving man I have ever known. I was a very shy, insecure person until I met him. He gave me confidence in myself. I loved and adored him but did not appreciate how much I worshipped him until it was too late. A year before my darling died I discussed with him that if one of us became terminally ill, we should go together,

because our love was so special, we could not live without one another. Ron would not discuss this seriously. He was such an optimist.

My darling, you will never know how much that last night, 12 May 1997, meant to me. My darling sweetheart lying there. Giving him the 'Kiss of Life'. Phoning paramedics. I kept my sweetheart alive. They found a pulse. I phoned you. You were able to say 'goodbye' to a very special Daddy. The vision of that night has haunted me for over a year – I could not believe my sweetheart had slipped away to heaven and left me alone. There were so many people waiting to welcome him; darling Margaret, Jack & Nannie, Grandma Hird. Everyone who loved him (the real people I mean).

Without my sweetheart my life is empty. In dreams he is with me but I have to cope with nightmare days without my love. You will never know how much I love and miss your Daddy, Laura. He was my life.

Laura, the house and any money are yours – enjoy them, sorry you have a lot to sort out. Look under mattress.

Darling, could you make sure a few of my books go to Gwen's son. Gwen, Val, Grace, Margaret Willins, Evelyn to have a choice of a keepsake – jewellery, paintings, trinkets, etc. Plants for Jonathan Gibsone. (They have all tried to comfort me in the past year.) The rest is yours, my darling. Dad and I love you and are proud of you. Be good to Alec.

Love Mumsie.

Bye xx

I arranged for mum's funeral to take place where dad and herself had been married and where I had been christened, in the Lawnmarket she grew up in, at St Giles' Cathedral. Mum was very close to the female minister there who had been a huge support when dad was ill and after he died. I asked her to conduct the service and for a piece by Chopin to be played on the piano. I was too upset to read anything at mum's funeral. St Giles' was packed. It was the beginning of the Festival, a time when mum used to love to go back to the High Street and see the street performers. She would have liked to see them outside the church. It would have tickled her pink.

On mum and dad's wedding anniversary the following year, Jonathan, Alec and myself took mum's ashes up to the rowan tree in the Pentlands to put beside dad, as she'd requested. It is a beautiful spot with the dark southern side of the Pentland Hills in the background. When I go there, I don't feel sad, but like they are with me. I talk to them. I sense them in the grass, the tree, the flowers round about me. It is our new home.

Dear Mum

Dear Mum

Amongst the many things I found in the house after I managed to work up the courage to come back after you'd gone, was one of many cardboard boxes full of photographs. The one full of the photos of you and dad on the happy holidays you spent together after I went away to study. The one you'd written 'DO NOT THROW AWAY OR I WILL HAUNT YOU' boldly on the side.

There was no need. You know I'm a compulsive hoarder, just like you were. You remember the letters, Christmas cards, notes, mementos, from every point of my life that filled the boxes in my bedroom (the room I now use as an office), taking up the same space that used to annoy you. 'Get rid of some of that junk or I'll have to sell the piano to make space,' you used to say. All this and more now lies in piles, overstuffed shelves, spilling out of drawers – a vast, random archive of memories. And now, I have inherited all your precious letters, photographs, elocution certificates, programmes, books, knick-knacks etc. that you lovingly collected over the course of your life, to add to them.

I never produced a grandchild for you both. You never, ever put any pressure on me to do so. When I die, there's no way I can guarantee what will happen to that precious box of photos, your other mementos, my own memories or your letters to me. Our clutter, as others might class it.

Where do our lives go? The first flat dad and you bought together, the same one I was brought up and live in now was built in 1899. My life here began in December 1966, yours just a few months earlier. Where is the evidence of the families who lived here before? Where did their mementos go?

I've been back living in the house since a few weeks after I last saw you. I still find myself talking out loud to you both sometimes. I have that painting an ex of yours did of you staring at me from the hall as I sit at my computer. The one that's got the lipstick marks on it where I used to kiss it when I was wee. I sleep in your old bedroom, where you used to read me stories and poems and dad used to sing to me. Jean and Norrie are still up the stairs and always look out for me. Apart from that, nearly all our old neighbours, aside from Aileen across the road, are away. I think there's probably more English people living in the street now than there were in London when I was at polytechnic.

The family are all fine and miss you very much. Ian and Alan are still working hard and their business is thriving. Alan's dad, Bobby, passed away some time ago but I expect you already know that. No doubt you are all making him very welcome. I've had some lovely nights down at their house with Ian showing off his culinary skills, or else we go out to restaurants to 'test-drive' them so Ian and Alan can recommend the best ones to guests. You and dad would love it. Sometimes Ian looks so like you, it's almost as if I can see you gazing out at me. It's the same with Morag. It gives me a warm feeling to still see a little of you in them both. One day outside the house a few months ago, an elderly lady stopped me and said 'June?' then apologised and said she'd thought I was someone else, so there must be a little bit of you in me as well. A bloody big bloody-fucking-special bit I'd say.

Morag, Bob and the girls are doing well. Morag has seven grandchildren now, one of whom is Nicky's who you/they sadly never got the chance to meet. Morag's been really kind to me. She always pops over at Christmas with a gift and sends me a card on 7 August. This year she gave me a lovely framed picture of dad and you in grandma and pappa's back green in Whitson in 1962 and a really sexy one of you that she'd had processed from slides. They look like they were taken yesterday. She's getting a lot of her old slides converted into photos and has invited me over to see them. Lauren emails me sometimes and still talks about you. She remembers all the stories you used to tell her and Mark. Lauren studied my novel as part of her Highers. I thought you'd be chuffed about that. I was really touched. She wants to go into dentistry but nobody seems to think it's a very good idea. I told her to go for it, there's lots of opportunities, it's very well paid and people will always have sair teeth. I knew that's what you'd probably have told her, so I passed it on.

Jonathan takes me to visit the tree on Mother's Day each year. It is growing well but we're still waiting on its first burst of rowanberries. We always plant fresh daffodils then go and sit in the garden at the cottage where those wonderful parties took place, listen to songs from musicals and raise a glass to Margaret, Jack, Sylvia, dad and yourself. Jonathan really misses you too. He still gets excited when he talks about the concerts you used to go to during the early Edinburgh Festivals. We never did find the programmes though. He sends his love.

I'm sorry I've not managed to pass on the mementos you requested to all your friends yet. A few I have but I'm afraid I fell out of touch with others in the months after you left. I felt so ashamed and embarrassed at the way I'd acted in front of some of them when I visited you at the hospice and before. I hope they can forgive me and that this book can be a way in which we can get back in touch and fulfil your wishes. I'm hoping everyone will come to the launch and we can celebrate you together.

Canongate absolutely love your writing. They said if you were still here they'd sign you up tomorrow. What do you think of that? You are going to be published alongside so many of your favourite writers – Burns, Robert Louis Stevenson. Lewis-bloody-Grassic Gibbon. And me, I suppose. I can't express how proud I am that I'm going to have the same publisher as JUNE HIRD.

I'm so glad you were still here when my first book was published so I could finally say 'Mum, I've done it.' But I've really missed telling you about the subsequent journeys my writing has taken me on – visiting Russia on a Scottish Writers' Tour and being invited to tea with Boris

Pasternak's niece (and getting the chance to tell her you'd named me after Lara in *Doctor Zhivago*). Having dinner at Pushkin's house. Travelling to Malta and visiting the home of a wonderfully gregarious and charismatic Count, which was crammed with the most incredible treasures and paintings which I know would have made you cry with joy like it did me (the moment I've missed you most so far). All the tales of the new friends I've made on Arvon courses, readings, writing workshops and through the website. The stories you'd waited all your life to hear me tell you. The good bits that had always seemed to elude me before.

I hope you can understand my desire to share your wonderful letters. They are too good to keep to myself. They are precious moments of a life that I always enjoyed sharing, even if a lot of the time it didn't seem that way. From sitting around in London with my college friends, laughing and crying together at your brilliant insights and the little idiosyncrasies of your and dad's everyday life. The way that 'dour wee bugger' became a catchphrase for us all at the time. Whether you were encouraging me, or pushing me, or telling it to me straight, or talking to me like your little baby bear, these letters bring you back so vividly, almost like you and dad are standing there beside me. Every time I look through them I can hear you reading them to me, just like you used to read to me when I was a wee girl.

I published some of your stories and holiday diaries on my website and boy, you would have been over the moon with the rapturous responses asking for more from mothers, daughters, fathers, sons all over the world. I wonder which ones you'd have ended up starting corresponding with yourself. Which ones you'd have become lifelong friends with. I wonder what a compulsive communicator like yourself would have made of email and Messenger. Honestly, it's just like having lodgers. Making friends and sharing ideas and passions with people all over the world. Except you don't have to make breakfast (and don't get paid . . .). Even if you'd hated it, you would have responded to some of your 'fans' I'm sure. You still have enough Andrex notepaper to last several life-times.

You wouldn't believe how few people actually write proper letters these days. It makes yours even more special. Everyone seems to communicate through email or mobile phones. You can even make international phone calls on a computer for free now. You'd be on it all the time. Remember on dad's birthday when I phoned his brother Dougie in Canada from the flat in McLeod Street and dad spoke to him for the first time in 27 years? I hope they have had the chance to be reunited properly now. Did they have telephones in heaven in the end? If so, when are you going to call? Or is it you in the afternoons when the phone rings and there's no-one there? If it is, I'm really sorry for shouting 'I DON'T CARE WHAT YOU'RE SELLING – I DON'T WANT IT!' (and worse) sometimes.

I think about dad and you all the time – wondering what advice you'd give me in new situations I find myself in;

what you'd make of the friends and people I've met since I saw you last. There are so many films I know you would have loved and songs you never got the chance to hear. That Gershwin CD you bought me in Bulgaria that I didn't play until you were gone always makes me cry because you both would have absolutely loved it.

Why didn't I ask dad and you more questions? You would have answered anything. You would have loved that I'd bothered to ask. When I lost you both, my mind was flooded with thousands of things I should have asked, that I'd always wanted to know but stupidly believed you'd always be around to answer.

Why didn't you have more confidence in your writing? In yourself? You always talked about writing a book and asked if I'd ever write a book about you. I hope you approve of how I've done it, and why I chose to do it this way. Your letters express the mum and woman you really were far better than I ever could. That incredible way you drift seamlessly between sentimentality, dry wit, romanticism, a wee bit manipulation (you have to admit), lovely silliness, heartbreak and compassion is just so completely you. Plus the beautiful honesty of your letters gave me the confidence to be honest about myself, my lifelong faults and about how badly I often treated dad and you (and other people) over the years (and since). There's no way I can ever make up for that. How could I? But please believe me, everything I did was not through lack of love, but too much of it – in both directions.

Oh mum, I'm getting like you. Now I've started to write

to you, I don't want to stop. I'm going to have to get going and read through everything again, ready to meet my editor tomorrow for the final meeting before the book is typeset. I just wanted to let you know how bloody proud I am of you. When Canongate told me they wanted to publish *Dear Laura* I was like dad skipping around Lauriston Place the day I was born. 'My mum's going to have her book published. Everybody listen to her name – JUNE HIRD – because you are going to be hearing a lot more from her!!' Canongate have agreed that a percentage from each book sold will be donated to the hospice. I thought that's what you'd want.

Oh well mum. I have this weird sensation now that I'm back down in London writing to you up here in Edinburgh. I guess that's because you've never gone away. Or dad. I carry you both about in my heart every day of my life. I miss you but still feel you are very close to me. Even if this is not the case I will keep believing it until I see you both again (if they'll let me in!!).

In the meantime I'll meet you both under the rowan tree next Mother's Day.

All my love, as ever and always,

Laura xxx

P.S. One last word (the one I always forgot to say) – thanks.

APPENDIXES

Characters

Ian: My mum's younger brother. Ian worked his way up over his life and now runs a successful guest house and apartments in Edinburgh with his partner, Alan. Wicked sense of humour, likes to enjoy himself, but I often worry he's going to work himself into the ground. I'm very close to Ian and can talk to him about absolutely anything. Know he'll probably gossip about it afterwards, but don't really mind any more.

Alan: My uncle's partner with whom he runs the guest house and apartments. His father, Bobby (sadly now deceased) and mother May were great fun and mum and dad always used to enjoy their company. Get on very well with Alan. Again, I can tell him anything and he will just laugh.

Alan B: My friend since we first met when working together in Rae Macintosh (Music) Ltd in about 1984. Mum loved him and was delighted I had a friend who was also interested in classical music, musicals etc. and used to love when he brought his clarinet or flute round and we would play duets, with me on the piano. She didn't like it so much when I'd phone up late and drunk throughout the '80s after a night in Fire Island or the Laughing Duck and ask if Alan could stay as he'd missed his last bus home (he lived with his parents in Livingston at the time). Despite a few fall-outs we are still good friends. Having travelled extensively, Alan is currently back in Scotland working as an artist and at an Arts Centre in West Lothian.

Eleanor: Friend who studied music at Edinburgh University in the mid to late '80s.

Anne: My best friend in my last two years at school and into my thirties. A great friend with whom I shared a passion for films and culture. I was also very close to her brother Mark, who took me to the Irvine Welsh reading at the Filmhouse which encouraged me to send my first story to Kevin Williamson. Love her parents Maimie and Alan – great people who were both very kind to me when I was suffering from depression. Maimie sadly died in 2005. Anne was great fun but was also a very stabilising influence in my life because of her honesty, loyalty and general sense of decency. Now married to Gary and working as a PA.

Bob: My friend/lover prior to/occasionally during my time studying in London. Worked for an airline at the time and would fly up to visit me in Edinburgh every few months. Was a good deal older than me (thirty-one years) but mum was happy as he had a good job and I don't think I ever admitted to her he was that old. They never met as he was only ever in Edinburgh overnight and generally stayed in hotels (apart from one time he stayed at mum's when they were on holiday).

Nikki (The Bairn): My youngest cousin with whom I was good friends when we were younger.

Auntie Margaret: Mum's best friend. Margaret was a retired schoolteacher and a great friend to mum, dad and myself. Like Jack, not a blood relative, but back then children generally called their parents' friends 'auntie' and 'uncle' to retain some form of respect. Margaret and mum used to love 'doing' the jumble sales and charity shops on Saturday afternoons and we had some great holidays in the Highlands (Margaret was originally from Inverness), Borders, etc. with them when I was young. Margaret also took me out for cake and juice and lent a shoulder to cry on over the course of my life. Margaret was someone I could talk to in complete confidentiality, even though she was so close to mum. A warm, lively, colourful lady. Died in 1992.

Uncle Jack: Husband of Margaret, Jack was a former journalist (at one time had his own column in the *Edinburgh Post*) and songwriter (Fats Waller recorded one of his songs, 'Smoke Dreams of You'). Jack was a formidable, extremely intelligent, charming man who died soon after his beloved Margaret in 1992. Mum and dad's ashes are planted under a rowan tree in his family's graveyard in Old Pentland.

Sylvia: Jack's sister. Widow of Martin Secker (of Secker and Warburg who first published *Lady Chatterley's Lover*).

Wonderful woman full of stories about the Bloomsbury Group, who would regularly attend parties held in the garden at the cottage in the Pentlands. Well into her seventies, she would get the train up to Edinburgh from Berwick to see art films at the Filmhouse that were never on down there. She and mum loved exchanging stories.

Jim: An elderly gentleman from Kent who first stayed with us as a lodger one summer with his wife, who subsequently died. Used to come up and visit and we'd go down there to see him. Mum called him Peter Pan and he called her Wendy. I think at times they truly convinced themselves this was the case. They were avid correspondents and I still have hundreds of letters they wrote to each other as Peter and Wendy. Used to send me £5 each month when I was a student in London. He died in about 1992.

Nannie: One of my grandfather's (on mum's side) cousins, Nannie was a real character in every sense of the word. A tiny woman with a huge personality, she wore elaborate, brightly coloured clothes and had an extremely infectious laugh and wicked sense of humour. Devoted to the Catholic Church she would light candles for us if we were unhappy or in trouble. Her biggest claim to fame was the time the priest was in her house, spilt tea on his trousers and had to put them on a chair in front of the fire to dry off. She took great satisfaction in her self-imposed moniker – 'The only woman to have got the breeks off a priest'.

Pappa: Mum's dad, James. My closest friend when

I was young, bought me my first mouth organ. A blacksmith by trade, euphonium player, one-time Stalinist, huge fan of Gandhi and the first person I ever met who did yoga. I used to love helping him plant vegetables in his garden, going to collect sheep's 'pirls' to make fertiliser, going to brass-band competitions and miners' gala days. A complex, loving man who was sometimes prone to depression. Used to say he was taking me out for walks on a Sunday, then would take me to the Wheatsheaf and bring me out a lemonade while he went inside for a pint. I found it all very exciting. He was also an extremely gifted carpenter and was forever making dolls' houses, theatres, farms and zoos for the kids in the family.

Grandma: Mum's mother, Annie Hamilton. A former dinner lady, grandma was one of the finest bakers I've ever met. When we visited her and pappa on a Sunday at their flat in Whitson, she used to home-bake apple pies, Victoria sponges, fruit cake, shortbread, etc. I used to go out with mum, grandma and pappa on Saturday afternoons when I was wee, either down Leith Walk for a bacon roll under the bridge that isn't there any more, or down the Southside, or along Portobello Promenade to the 'strawberry and vanilla' toilets at Eastfield. Died shortly after her beloved Jimmy in November 1986.

Colin: Boarder who stayed in the front room at mum's for a while during the time I was studying in London.

Cam: Owner of a large guest house in the centre of Edinburgh where dad and I sometimes used to work. She would also send us guests when her guest house was full. Family friend with her husband, Jim. Nice lady with the most illegible handwriting I've ever seen. Mum, dad and I used to have fun trying to decipher letters and Christmas cards. Often referred to as 'Lilo Lil' as mum used to joke that dad was her toy boy when he went to work there.

June S: Mum's friend and work colleague from the Polwarth Medical Practice.

Auntie Morag: My mum's younger sister. Has lived just along the road since I was born. Married to Bob, with three daughters – Nikki, Pam and Carole. Always the first family in the street to get the latest new things – first colour telly I ever saw, first tape recorder, first caravanette, first freezer (ice cream in your own house!), first holiday to Florida, etc. Morag always tried to do what she thought was best for mum, but this could sometimes encroach on dad and me and cause unintentional hurt and conflict. Has a brilliantly wicked sense of humour. Devoted to her family. Since mum died has always sent me a much appreciated 'Thinking of You' card on the anniversary of mum's death and a present at Christmas.

Carole: My oldest cousin on mum's side. Married to Gary, with three kids. Mum was particularly close to her eldest son and daughter, Lauren and Mark.

Andy: My on/off boyfriend between 1983 and 1988.

Didn't hit it off with mum and dad. The only time they met him he turned up drunk. I've never known my dad to hate someone so much. Although he drank a lot, Andy was a gentle man, an ageing hippy, and I used to enjoy visiting the various bars of Stockbridge (where he lived), Leith and the hotel bars of the New Town with him in the days when bars still closed on a Sunday afternoon. After visiting Thailand in 1990, he fell in love with the place and lived there, as far as I know, until his death in 2003.

Jonathan: One of Margaret and Jack's three sons, Jonathan remains a great friend. Was very good to mum after dad died, visiting, taking her for runs, reminiscing, etc. They shared a love of the music of the '20s and '30s and mum used to love telling him about all the concerts she'd gone to in the opening years of the Edinburgh International Festival. I've always felt Jonathan was born in the wrong time and would have been happier if he was the age he is now in the 1920s.

David: My boyfriend in 1989–90. First man I ever lived with. Still a good friend. Studied philosophy and subsequently went on to complete a PhD in Continental Philosophy. David wrote poetry and plays which I used to type up and send off to literary magazines for him, which was where I first became interested in the underground literary scene. David was also in a band called the Sawdust Caesars. We lived together until 1990. His family lived in a beautiful cottage just outside Melton Mowbray where he banged drums and played guitar in the holidays. Currently writes and occasionally lectures in philosophy.

Dennis Nilsen: Former civil servant who murdered fifteen men between 1978 and 1983 in London. Sentenced to life imprisonment in 1983. I corresponded with him for a year as part of a project on artistic representations of crimes I produced as an essay during my finals at polytechnic. Nilsen was a prolific correspondent who would send me poetry, etc.

Audrey: Nannie's niece.

Pam: My middle cousin, on mum's side. In the late 1970s I heard punk music for the first time via her then boyfriend's Sham 69 album. Married to Paul with three kids.

Mandy and her two sisters: Three sisters with whom I was at primary school who were singers and, I believe, were once on *Opportunity Knocks*. Used to also regularly sing in talent contests at the Ross Bandstand.

Dr W: One of the GPs from the Polwarth Medical Practice who mum loved working with and with whom she got on really well. One of the 'old school' of GPs who really cared about the patients and consequently had queues of them every time he was working. Think mum always had a bit of a crush on him. Was good to see him at her funeral.

Tommy: Mum's boyfriend before she met dad. Lived in Glasgow and was a lecturer at Strathclyde University. Mum's first big love affair.

Mark: My best friend between the ages of three and

eleven. Lived next door with his family and younger sister, Michelle. I used to go and play with his Action Men. He had all the accessories and loads of outfits. Also had Scalextric. Used to go out on our bikes to Hermitage of Braid, Colinton Dell, along the canal, etc. Also used to put on mini-musicals with him and the other kids that lived locally, play football and hide up trees from the Gorgie Jungle Gang.

Douglas: My friend Anne's boyfriend for a few months while I was a student. Kind, warm guy who memorably stood up for my dad at a family party once.

Heather: Jim's daughter who corresponded regularly with mum and we visited her and her family once when we were down in Kent seeing Jim. Used to always send us well-thought-out and unusual birthday and Christmas presents.

Nick: Son of Margaret and Jack. Always got on well with mum, dad and me. Worked in advertising and is married to Helen.

Helen: Wife of Nick. Nick and Helen were regulars at the parties at the cottage.

David G: Margaret and Jack's eldest son. Lives in England but came to a few of the parties at the family's cottage.

Sue: One of the students who took digs with us in the front room when I was growing up.

Claire: My best friend when I was a student, and still a good friend. Now married and living in London where she manages a legal bookshop. Visited me a couple of times in Edinburgh and got on very well with mum and dad.

Karen: Audrey's (Nannie's niece) daughter.

Anya: Mum's psychologist following the heart surgery.

Dr H: One of the GPs at the medical practice our family went to.

Grandma Hird: My dad's mother who lived in Wardlaw and died in 1969, when I was two. Remember being washed in her sink overlooking the railway and the big chest of drawers she used to let me rifle through which was full of odds and ends that fascinated me. Dad's dad (Douglas) died while his mother was pregnant with him in 1931, so they never met.

Gwen: Friend of mum's who used to take mum out for runs down to Peebles for lunch etc., even when she was quite ill and they needed to take an oxygen cylinder in the car with them. Mum loved this because towards the end of her life the rest of us were too worried to take her anywhere. Visited mum regularly in hospital/ the hospice and was at the party mum held at the house for her friends the night before she went into the hospice for the final time. A character.

Val: Mum's friend who used to visit her regularly. In last months of mum's life she took mum on holiday to Canterbury with mum in the wheelchair. (Val, Gwen, Evelyn, Grace and my mum used to call themselves 'the Golden Girls'.)

Grace: Friend of mum's who she met when they were both in hospital at the same time during their teens.

They enjoyed going out dancing and on holidays together when they were young, and were together at the Cavendish the night mum met dad. Both Grace and her husband, David, were a great support and they are still friends of mine.

Margaret W: Friend of mum's whose daughters I was at school with. Used to pop along to mum's each day and make her lunch when mum was at home latterly and confined to bed. Regularly visited mum in hospital.

Evelyn: Friend of mum's and daughter of my pappa's best friend when he lived in Whitson Terrace. Grew up in same street as mum and her family in Whitson and was a great support to mum after dad died.

Alec: My partner in 1994–99. Former prison officer who got on very well with mum and dad. Dad used to go round to visit him at our flat in McLeod Street to talk about horses and football, but always kept his jacket on. Alec stayed with me at the hospice during the last four days of mum's life. He called her 'June Doll'.

Further Writing

The following are examples of mum's writing from when she was a member of a writing group at the Adult Learning Project in the mid-1990s. In them she talks about growing up in Edinburgh's Lawnmarket, and her feelings for dad, Nannie, Margaret, Jack and myself.

OLD TOWN STREETS

Whenever I feel nostalgia for my happy childhood days, I only need to take a stroll from Edinburgh Castle to St Giles' Cathedral. Not only do memories come flooding back, but I also feel a sense of communion with the famous and infamous historical characters who once walked in the paths I am treading.

I was born in my grandmother's house in the Lawnmarket. I can remember, as a child, carefully running down the staircase from her house, avoiding the narrow parts of the steps, which tapered into the spiral staircase. I had been told that spiral staircases had been constructed to facilitate fencing duels, enabling the people concerned to dodge their opponent.

The ghosts of the past were Gran's immediate neighbours. Brodie's Close, next door, had been the home of the notorious Deacon Brodie (of Dr Jekyll and Mr Hyde fame). My gran told me that during some reconstruction work, she had seen workmen uncover a secret staircase which Deacon Brodie had used during his nocturnal misdeeds. Robert Burns had stayed in the house opposite Gran's during one of his visits to Edinburgh. In the Upper Bow, Major Weir, the Edinburgh warlock, and his sister Grizel, were reputed to have lived and tales of his ghost being seen riding his stallion over Edinburgh Castle used to give me many a sleepless night.

At Riddle's Court there is a beautiful Italian balcony, where I used to stand and dream that I was Juliet, waiting to hear Romeo whisper, 'But soft, what light through yonder window breaks?'

Now grandmother's window – it was an experience to behold. One could watch soldiers, pipers and military bands marching to and from the Castle, during the royal residence at Holyrood Palace.

I also used to watch the quaintly dressed fishwife with her creel, sitting outside Deacon Brodie's Tavern, selling mussels and buckies. The buckie is a small curly shellfish, sold in its shell, and extracted with a pin. The mussels were served on a saucer, salt and vinegar added to taste and delicately eaten in the street with the aid of a teaspoon.

From his pitch opposite, near the Sheriff Courthouse, I would watch and listen to the news-vendor's strange call 'Spatchet News'. French? One may well ask, as in the Royal Mile call of yesteryear, 'Gardyloo'. No, he was selling the *Evening News* and *Evening Dispatch*.

Saturday was a special day. Gran gave me my Saturday penny. I had the difficult decision to make whether to spend it in Granny Meikle's shop, near Riddle's Court – her home-made treacle doddles were delicious and kept me chewing for ages – or alternatively, I could enter the inner sanctum of Alex Ferguson Ltd, Confectioners, at the junction of George IV Bridge and Lawnmarket. Oh, those lavish fitted tartan carpets and the charming assistants also dressed in tartan.

The sign outside proudly stated, 'By Royal Appointment'. I wondered nervously at the door if royalty enjoyed their Edinburgh Rock as much as I did. 'A pennyworth of broken rock, please,' was my usual, shy order, hoping they would include a bit of ginger rock in the deftly twisted paper poke.

A few doors away on George IV Bridge was the site of The Old City Buffet. A memorial seat to the owners, Mr and Mrs William Wilson, who were a delightful couple, is now the only reminder.

They would allow children to join their parents in the small lounge bar.

Sometimes on a Saturday my dad would say, 'Don't tell mum,' and would take me to the 'Buffet', order a pint for himself and delicious pie with gravy and a fizzy lemonade for me. It was a favourite haunt of members of the court and the press too. I loved the atmosphere and secrecy of it all.

My little tour ends at St Giles' Cathedral, so much a part of my past. Within its ancient portals my parents were married, I was baptised and married and our daughter was baptised. Our wedding service was conducted by the Rev. Harry Whitley. This pleasant, compassionate and controversial man, with his warm smile and twinkling eyes, was like a bright spring sunshine within the sombre, grey cathedral walls. I shall always treasure the memory of this wonderful man with his delightful family.

Some of the landmarks have changed but enough remain to provide me with a happy walk in the past.

THE BEST TIME OF DAY

In all our years together the only subject about which you and I disagreed was the best time of the day. As I snuggled into your arms at night I would say 'evening', knowing that you and I were together, safe and warm until morning.

As I drowsily awoke, the delicious aroma of freshly made coffee and hot buttered toast teased my taste buds. Your smiling newly shaved face materialising to my half-closed eyelids. A kiss and a whiff of your after-shave and, 'wakey wake, a new day awaits us'.

Even on holiday after dancing until the wee small hours you would still be up at daybreak eager to seek pastures new.

That last morning, I made the toast and coffee for you. You were eating breakfast as I made some coffee for myself. When I came to join you, you had gone, half of the warm coffee still in the cup.

He will not come back, they said, but I could not believe them. Your electric razor still plugged in. Your smart new clothes still hanging in place.

You could not leave like that, so many plans still unfulfilled. I only know that without you there is no best time of day.

NAN: EIGHTY-NINE YEARS YOUNG

Nan will be eighty-nine years old in May. Old, did I say? Never. Although Nan boasts of being a year older than the present century and having lived during the reign of six monarchs, I always think of her as eighty-nine years young. I have always been amazed at Nan's quick, agile brain, amazing memory and beautiful singing voice. Apart from that, her pride in her appearance, hair always perfect, an eye for fashion. Those qualities, combined with a compassionate heart and an infectious sense of humour make her a very special person. She was prompter in a production of *A Midsummer Night's Dream* in which I played Helena. When the twenty-year-old

Puck fell ill at the last minute, Nan, in her mid-sixties, volunteered to play the part — somersaults, cartwheels and all. The show was a brilliant success, Puck being given very special mention.

Nan's grit probably stemmed from her childhood. The eldest and only daughter in a family of six. She was a brilliant scholar, with hopes of a teaching career when her beloved dad was enlisted for the First World War in 1914. Poor Dad. Tom was not given the chance to be a hero. Whilst returning to the Front following compassionate leave after his youngest son died of tuberculosis, he opened the train compartment window and accidentally fell onto the path of an oncoming express train.

Mother bereft and four remaining little brothers, Nan took control, left school and career behind and started work as a shop assistant to support them all at fifteen. At twenty, things were still very tight financially. Two more little brothers had died of tuberculosis. She needed a lot of money in a hurry and set off, steerage, to America. Within a year she was personal lady's maid to the daughter of a millionaire. Dollars galore were sent home. Mum was solvent at last. Every two years, Nan had to return home or become a nationalised American subject which she did not wish. She returned home three times in all, bearing the millionaire's 'cast-offs'. Mum now had pure silk undies and fox furs.

On the third visit home, she met Colin, married him and settled down in her home town of Edinburgh. Still looking after her beloved mum and seeing the two remaining brothers happily married, she also continued a full-time job and was the mainstay of all the charity work for the local Catholic Church, of which she was a devout member.

Alas, Colin, Nan's mum, her brothers and all her generation are dead. She lives in sheltered housing, in an immaculate little flat. Crippled by arthritis, sight almost gone. So frail and bird-like, when she ventures to her nearby chapel for mass or to burn candles, she is quite often blown over by a sudden Edinburgh south-east wind.

However, the valiant spirit is still there. When we visit we must be prepared to stay for ages to hear her wonderful tales. When we have problems, she always says, 'Never mind, Nannie will light a candle,' and we feel everything will be fine. I hope Nannie (my pet name for her) will reach her century, for the world would be a dull place without her inspiration.

CEUD MILE FAILTE

She was sitting alone with her memories – a luxury that no-one could take away from her. They were all she had left but she considered herself rich that they were all so happy. Happy memories are like rainbows, they glisten and glow.

Tonight she smiled as she remembered the day Margaret and Jack returned from Inverness with a little present for her darling husband and herself. It was a little wall plate with the greeting 'ceud mile failte'. 'That means a hundred thousand welcomes in Gaelic,' said Margaret. 'You must hang it inside at the door to welcome people.'

She was right. The house was always full of visitors from all over the world and friends always seemed to drop in.

Margaret and Jack, her husband and she were such great friends. They were a quartet whose every outing was an adventure.

She remembered sadly the day a gust of wind blew the 'ceud mile failte' plate to a hundred thousand pieces.

Now her husband, Margaret and Jack are gone. She is all that is left of the quartet. She firmly believes that they are waiting with a hundred thousand welcomes for her in Heaven.

In the meantime she is going to summon on her feeble strength to visit Inverness to try to find a replacement 'ceud mile failte' plate in the hope that when a hundred thousand welcomes beckon again the people who used to enjoy their hospitality may return once more.

LAURA (1987)

There had not always been conflict between Laura and her Mum. The early years and early teens had been so idyllic. Her mother had guided her along the artistic path, which she had loved. As there would only be one child, during the pregnancy the mother had read her favourite poems and played her favourite music to her child 'in utero'. To her delight the little girl loved poetry, loved drawing and by the age of six was already having piano lessons, at which she excelled. By sixteen she had 'A' passes in English, art and music Highers and was about to take her final grade in piano. Her future seemed secure.

Then Mum noticed a change in Laura, a feeling of resentment: she would lock her door to keep her Mum out, accused her of prying and trying to run her life. Laura started staying out late and frequenting pubs. 'Could she be on drugs?' the mother thought. Laura's friends assured her she was not but added that Laura was a very confused girl. The arguments they had did nothing to further understanding between mother and daughter. They only widened the gaps of distrust. The only hope occasionally would be a little hand-made card saying, 'Sorry, I love you, why do I hurt you?'

The last straw was reached one weekend shortly before the final piano examination. Laura announced, 'That is it. I am abandoning music.' She closed the piano lid and that was it, no more scales, Czerny exercises, Chopin *Nocturnes*. 'It is a phase,' friends would say. 'She loves music too much.' A few weeks later the art books and paints were thrown out, followed a week later by all the poems and short stories she had written. 'You are destroying a part of yourself,' the mother screamed. 'Your own creative self.' The tears did not help the conflict. They only added fuel to the fire.

Laura presently took a poorly paid job in an office, a job she hated. She ate too much and became very over-weight. For four years she remained in this state of creative limbo. Mother and daughter just did not talk the same language any more – a dividing line of conflict was there constantly. Mum was sure Laura would move into a flat any day.

Suddenly, Laura started to diet, draw some pictures again and, miracle of miracles, returned to practising piano. 'Ours is not to reason why,' thought Mum. Laura was becoming her little girl again. Arriving home un-expectedly one day she discovered the reason. The strains of a piano playing 'Home Sweet Home' and above the sound of a flute. The usually locked door was open, Laura looked flushed and pretty, smiling at the handsome young flautist. 'Oh Mummy darling, how lovely to see you. I would like you to meet Alan.'

The conflict was over at last. Love had triumphed and unlocked the beautiful artistic soul trapped in its own heart.

ACKNOWLEDGMENTS

Many thanks to my agent, Stan at Jenny Brown Associates; and to Karen McCrossan, Helen Bleck, Jamie Byng and everyone at Canongate Books for their enthusiasm, hard work and support. Also my appreciation to friends and family who have offered encouragement and advice on the task over the last couple of years.

Laura Hird was born in Edinburgh, where she still lives. June Hird, her mother, was also Edinburgh born and bred, and her letters to her daughter form the heart of *Dear Laura*. Laura has written three other books – *Hope and Other Urban Tales*, *Nail and Other Stories*, and her widely acclaimed novel, *Born Free*, which was shortlisted for the Whitbread First Novel Award and nominated for the Orange Prize. Two novellas have also appeared in the anthologies *Children of Albion Rovers* and *Rovers Return*. Her stories have appeared in publications throughout Europe and the USA.